The MYSTERY FANcier

**Volume 1   Number 6
November   1977**

THE MYSTERY FANCIER

Volume 1 Number 6
November 1977

TABLE OF CONTENTS

MYSTERIOUSLY SPEAKING 1
Raymond Chandler on Film: An Annotated Checklist,
    Part I, by Peter Pross 3
The Degeneration of Donald Hamilton, by George Kelley . 11
The Mysterious John Dickson Carr, by Larry L. French . . 13
The Nero Wolfe Saga, Part IV, by Guy M. Townsend. . . . 15
Pocket Books Checklist, 1-500, compiled by Hal Knott
    and Marvin Lachman 29
MYSTERY*FILE: Short Reviews by Steve Lewis: Crowe, *When
    They Kill Your Wife*; Maguire, *Scratchproof*; Hilton,
    Gamekeeper's Gallows; McCloy, *The Changeling Con-
    spiracy*; Rossiter, *The Murder Makers*; Drummond,
    The Necklace of Skulls; Stein, *Coffin Country*;
    Spain, *Death Goes on Skis*; Saxon, *A Run in Dia-
    monds*. 38
VERDICTS (More Reviews): Lathen, *By Hook or By Crook*
    (Broset); Simmons, *The Z Papers* (Broset); Heyer,
    They Found Him Dead (Broset); Gillis, *The Killers
    of Starfish* (Broset); Bloch, *The King of Terrors*
    (Wooster); Chandler, *Raymond Chandler Speaking*
    (Meyerson); Pronzini (ed.), *Midnight Specials*
    (Kelley); Axton, *Prison of Ice* (Kelley); Moyes,
    Black Widower (Townsend); Asimov, *Asimov's Mys-
    teries* (Townsend); Hamilton, *The Terrorizers*
    (Townsend); Lovesey, *A Case of Spirits* (Townsend);
    Childers, *The Riddle of the Sands* (Townsend); Delv-
    ing, *Smiling, the Boy Fell Dead*, *The Devil Finds
    Work*, *Die Like a Man* (Kelley); Collins, *Bait Money*,
    Blood Money, *The Broker*, *The Broker's Wife*, *The
    Dealer* (Kelley); Stark, *The Sour Lemon Score* (Meyer-
    son); Burley, *Three-Toed Pussy* (Meyerson); Sapir &
    Murphy, *Mafia Fix* (Meyerson); Stein, *Days of Mis-
    fortune* (Bakerman); Cohen, *The Corpse that Walked*
    (Shibuk); O'Donnell, *The Impossible Virgin* (Woos-
    ter) 42
THE DOCUMENTS IN THE CASE (Letters): David C. Ralph;
    Gerie Frazier; Bob Briney; Jeff Meyerson; Marv
    Lachman; Myrtis Broset; Larry French 55

    Subscription rates: Domestic first class mail, $7.50 per
year (6 issues); Overseas surface mail, $7.50; Over-
seas air mail, $12.00 (overseas subscribers please
pay in international money order, check drawn on
U.S. bank, or currency; no checks on foreign banks,
please). Make checks payable to Guy M. Townsend.
Subscriptions are by volume; people who subscribe in
mid-year have the option of receiving back issues or
delaying their subscription start-up until the first
number of the next volume. ISSN:0146-3160
The MYSTERY FANcier is edited and published by Guy M. Townsend, 1256 Pidgeon Perch Lane, Memphis, TN 38116, USA.
Deadline for January issue: 1 December 1977.

Copyright © 1977 by Guy M. Townsend
All rights reserved for contributors.

MYSTERIOUSLY SPEAKING...

Well, we've made it through a full volume, and I'm quite pleased with TMF's growth and progress. TMF now has 140 individual subscribers, and it was, at one time or another, being sold at three bookstores. My dealings with these outlets have, however, been uniformly disappointing--one shop (whose name I may reveal if it doesn't pay up soon) was in to me for $100 before I finally cut it off--so from no own TMF will be available by subscription only. Of course, some of you will choose not to subscribe to volume two, but I'm fairly confident that TMF will hang on to at least the 100 subscribers needed to break even on the cost of paper, ink and stencils.

This issue, though dated November, is being mailed out in mid-September, for which ridiculous behavior you are certainly due an explanation. Here it is. From mid-September through early-to-mid-December I will be out of the country, bumming around Great Britain and Ireland (and possibly Europe), so I had to get this issue out early if I was to get it out at all. The next issue, volume two, number one, will be dated January 1978 and will be out in January at the latest. HOWEVER, since I will not be able to cash any subscription checks until the end of the year, I ask that you HOLD OFF ON SENDING YOUR SUBSCRIPTION PAYMENTS FOR VOLUME TWO UNTIL YOU HAVE RECEIVED THE JANUARY ISSUE. Instead, if you wish to subscribe to volume two, send me a postcard. That way I'll know how many subscribers I have without screwing up your checking accounts. This is important: YOU WILL NOT RECEIVE TMF 2:1 UNLESS I RECEIVE A POSTCARD FROM YOU, so why not put this issue down for a minute and scratch off a note to me.

All mail addressed to me at 1256 Pidgeon Perch Lane will be held for me until my return, so don't wait around until December to send in your articles, reviews and letters of comment--you might forget, or even lose the manuscript.

This issue we are quite short on letters, though part of the fault is mine for pushing up the deadline without announcing the change. However, my experience is that most letters of comment arrive within a month of publication, so I doubt that my action will cut out many letters. If I have any bad vibes at all about TMF, it is about the paucity of letters of comment. I can't help thinking that TMF ought to be exciting more feedback if it was doing its job properly.

Not too much on hand right now for the next issue, but there's plenty of time yet and I look forward to coming back to a huge stack of articles, l.o.c.s, and maybe even--dare I hope?--a cover illustration or two. A couple of reviews have already trickled in, and Steve Lewis released some more stuff to me just too late for this issue. He has also sent me a number of short notices of recent releases, which I hope to be able to use before they get stale. Problem is, TMF is limited to sixty pages until we start getting some ads to provide money for increasing the number of content pages. One other item that will appear in 2:1 will be Jeff Meyerson's index of books reviewed in TMF volume one.

SUBSCRIPTION RENEWALS

All subscriptions expire with this issue. Unless you contributed to one or more issues of volume one, you must pay the full subscription price to receive volume two. That price remains the same for domestic subscriptions—$7.50 for six issues via first class mail. There is a change for overseas subscriptions. For surface rate subscriptions the price drops from $9.00 to $7.50, and with the new format TMF is now available via air mail overseas for $12.00.

As announced in the Preview Issue, contributors to TMF are rewarded (however inadequately) for their efforts by receiving credit on their next year's subscription for each issue of the present volume in which their material has appeared. Below is a list of contributors to volume one. The numbers in parentheses indicate the issues to which they contributed, and the dollar amounts indicate how much they must pay for a subscription to volume two.

Adey (3)	$6.25	Kelley (1,2,4,5,6)	$1.25
Albert (1)	6.25	Lachman (PI,1,2,4,6)	1.25
Aucott (1)	6.25	Lewis (PI, 1-6)	0.00
Bakerman (5,6)	5.00	McAleer (1)	6.25
Banks (2,3,4)	3.75	McFarland (1)	6.25
Black (1)	6.25	Meltzer (4)	6.25
Briney (PI,1,3,5,6)	1.25	Mertz (4)	6.25
Broset (2,4,5,6)	2.50	Meyerson (1-6)	0.00
Butler (2,3)	5.00	Moffatt (1)	6.25
Clark (2)	6.25	Murray (1)	6.25
Cole (5)	6.25	Nevins (1-5)	1.25
Ekblaw (1)	6.25	Pross (1,5,6)	3.75
Frazier (6)	6.25	Ralph (6)	6.25
French (6)	6.25	Scott (PI,1-4)	1.25
Goldsmith (1)	6.25	Shibuk (1-6)	0.00
Goodrich (2)	6.25	Sorrell (1,5)	5.00
Groff (2)	6.25	Thompson (2)	6.25
Halpern (1)	6.25	Waterhouse (2)	6.25
Juri (5)	6.25	Williams (2,5)	5.00
Kabatchnik (1-5)	1.25	Wooster (2,4,5,6)	2.50

Three other people will receive volume two free in exchange for their own publications: John Ball, Iwan Hedman and David Hellyer.

My thanks go to every one of the above contributors, without whose help TMF would never have gotten past the Preview Issue. Special thanks go to Bob Briney, Amnon Kabatchnik, George Kelley, Marv Lachman, Steve Lewis, Jeff Meyerson, Mike Nevins, Art Scott and Charles Shibuk, who contributed to five or more issues and who, by their regularity, have practically become staff members of TMF.

RAYMOND CHANDLER ON FILM: AN ANNOTATED CHECKLIST
By Peter Pross

PART I
FILM ADAPTATIONS OF RAYMOND CHANDLER'S NOVELS

THE FALCON TAKES OVER. RKO Radil Pictures, Inc., 1942. 63 min., sd., b&w.* Based on the novel *Farewell, My Lovely* and the character created by Michael Arlen.

    Between 1941 and 1946, RKO Radio Pictures released thirteen black and white Falcon films as a motion picture series. Sanders was the star of the first four; the remaining balance featured Sanders' real life brother Tom Conway. In July 1941, Chandler's agent arranged a contract with RKO to film *Farewell, My Lovely* for $2,000. Chandler signed away virtually all other rights to RKO in what he later described as "a contract of almost unparallel stupidity on the part of my New York agent." THE FALCON TAKES OVER was released during May of 1942 with George Sanders as the debonaire antithesis of Philip Marlowe.

Credits
Producer	Howard Benedict
Director	Irving Reis
Screenplay	Lynn Root & Frank Fenton
Director of Photography	George Robinson
Music Director	C. Bakaleinikoff
Art Directors	Albert S. D'Agostino & F. M. Gray
Editor	Harry Marker

Cast
The Falcon	George Sanders
Ann Riordan	Lynn Bari
Mike O'Hara	James Gleason
Goldy Locke	Allen Jenkins
Diana Kenyon	Helen Gilbert
Moose Malloy	Ward Bond
Bates	Edward Cargan
Jessie Florian	Ann Revere
Lindsey Marriot	Hans Conreid
Jules Amthor	Turhan Bey
Laird Burnett	Selmer Jackson

TIME TO KILL. Twentieth Century Fox Film Corp., 1942. 5,479 ft., sd., b&w. Based on the novel *The High Window* and the character "Michael Shayne" created by Brett Halliday.

    The High Window was sold to Twentieth Century Fox for $3,500 and incorporated into an already established low budget (B) series. TIME TO KILL was released in January of 1943 as a Lloyd Nolan/Michael Shayne vehicle.

* sd.-sound; b&w-black & white; mm.-millimeter; min.-minutes

Credits

Producer	Sol M. Wurtzel
Director	Herbert I. Leeds
Screenplay	Clarence Upson Young
Music Director	Emil Newman

Cast

Michael Shayne	Lloyd Nolan
Merle	Heather Angel
Linda Conquest	Dorris Merrick
Louis Venter	Ralph Byrd
Lieut. Breeze	Richard Lane
Lois Morny	Sheila Bromley
Mrs. Murdock	Ethel Griffies
Leslie Murdock	James Seay
Phillips	Ted Hecht

MURDER MY SWEET. RKO Radio Pictures, Inc., 1945. 95 min., sd., b&w. Based on the novel *Farewell, My Lovely*.

MURDER MY SWEET was released January 10, 1945; the film was awarded the first Edgar presented by the Mystery Writers of America for best mystery film of the year. "For Raymond Chandler, as for Hammett, the background for the outbreak of violence is social corruption. Philip Marlowe, the private eyeeye, the man who seeks the truth, knows the big city but is not part of it; he is, despite appearances, incorruptable. Chandler regarded MURDER MY SWEET . . . as the most successful film adaptation of his novels, and thought that Dick Powell came closest to his conception of Marlowe. Directed in the brutal, fast style popular in the war years." (*Whodunit*)

Credits

Producer	Adrian Scott
Director	Edward Dmytryk
Screenplay	John Paxton
Music	Roy Webb
Music Director	C. Bakaleinikoff
Director of Photography	Harry J. Wild
Special Effects	Vernon L. Wilder
Editor	Joseph Noriega

Cast

Philip Marlowe	Dick Powell
Mrs. Grayle	Claire Trevor
Ann Grayle	Anne Shirley
Jules Amthor	Otto Kruger
Moose Malloy	Mike Mazurki
Mr. Grayle	Miles Mander
Marriott	Douglas Walton
Lieut. Randall	Don Douglas
Dr. Sonderborg	Ralf Harolde
Mrs. Florian	Esther Howard

THE BIG SLEEP. Warner Brothers Pictures, Inc., 1946. 114 min., sd., b&w, 35 mm. A Warner Brothers First National picture. From the novel by Raymond Chandler.

THE BIG SLEEP was released on August 31, 1946; Humphrey Bogart portrayed Chandler's private eye in an incredibly complicated thriller." "It takes place in the big city of displaced persons--the night city where sensation is all. The action is tense and fast, and the film catches the lurid Chandler atmosphere. The characters are a collection of sophisticated monsters--blackmailers, pornographers, apathetic society girls (Bacall and Martha Vickers are a baffling pair of spoiled sisters: the latter sucks her thumb), drug addicts, nymphomaniacs (a brunette Dorothy Malone seduces the hero in what must surely be record time), and murderers." (*Whodunit*)

Credits

Producer . . . . Howard Hawks
Director . . . . Howard Hawks
Screenplay . . . . William Faulkner,
                                           Leigh Brackett &
                                           Jules Furthman
Director of Photography . . . . Sid Hickox
Special Effects . . . . E. Roy Davidson &
                                           Warren E. Lynch
Art Director . . . . Carl Jules Weyl
Music . . . . Max Steiner
Music Director . . . . Leo F. Forbstein
Editor . . . . Christian Nyby

Cast

Philip Marlowe . . . . Humphrey Bogart
Vivian (Mrs. Regan) . . . . Lauren Bacall
Carmen Sternwood . . . . Martha Vickers
General Sternwood . . . . Charles Waldron
Eddie Mars . . . . John Ridgely
Norris . . . . Charles D. Brown
Bernie Ohls . . . . Regis Toomey
Joe Brody . . . . Louis Jean Heydt
Harry Jones . . . . Elisha Cook, Jr.
Canino . . . . Bob Steele
Agnes . . . . Sonia Darrin
Arthur Geiger . . . . Theodore Von Eltz
Mona Mars . . . . Peggy Knudsen
Carol Lundgren . . . . Tom Rafferty
Girl in Bookstore . . . . Dorothy Malone

THE LADY IN THE LAKE. Loew's Inc., 1946. Presented by Metro-Goldwyn-Mayer. Eleven reels, sd., b&w, 35 mm. Based on the novel by Raymond Chandler.

 Marlow's Christian name gained an extra "l" during the film adaptation of THE LADY IN THE LAKE which was released in January, 1947. One further item of interest is found in the film's credits which list Chrystal Kingsby as being played by Ellay Mort. Those familiar with the novel or with the French language should be able to figure out director Robert Montgomery's black humor. Chandler originally agreed to write the screenplay in order to keep it from being ruined by a hack writer. However, he left an incomplete script behind after thriteen weeks of work. "I didn't finish it," Chandler admitted, "and it is probably all bitched up by now (or perhaps I bitched it up), but after that one was over, I had to be hit on the head with a baseball bat to make me get out of a chair." Steve Fisher completed the script, and Chandler thought it was so bad he refused to have his name associated with the screenplay. ("Raymond Chandler and Hollywood")

Chandler also ridiculed the subjective camera technique employed by director/star Robert Montgomery. The camera was the detective's--and the spectator's--eyes, and the audience saw Marlowe only when he faced a mirror and at the end of the film. Despite Chandler's criticisms, the movie met a favorable audience and was well received by contemporary film critics.

Credits

Producer	George Haight
Director	Robert Montgomery
Screenplay	Steve Fisher
Special Effects	Arnold Gillespie
Director of Photography	Paul C. Vogel
Art Directors	Cedric Gibbons & Preston Ames
Music	David Snell
Editor	Gene Ruggiero

Cast

Phillip Marlowe	Robert Montgomery
Adrienne Fromsett	Audrey Totter
Lieut. DeGarmot	Lloyd Nolan
Captain Kane	Tom Tully
Derace Kingsby	Leon Ames
Mildred Haviland	Jayne Meadows
Chris Lavery	Dick Simmons
Eugene Grayson	Morris Ankrum
Mrs. Grayson	Kathleen Lockhart
Chrystal Kingsby	Ellay Mort

THE BRASHER DOUBLOON. Twentieth Century-Fox Film Corp., 1947. 72 min., sd., b&w, 35 mm. Based on the novel *The High Window*.

Released May 21, 1947, THE BRASHER DOUBLOON completed the 1940's quartet of Chandler's novel adaptations. The film was a low-budget production and is considered the least effective Marlowe film vehicle. THE BRASHER DOUBLOON, more than any other Marlowe film, most completely violates the spirit of Chandler, especially in the area of characterizations. Marlowe was provided with an overriding love interest in the person of Merle Davis. George Montgomery portrayed a hero who wasn't concerned with seeing justice done, (unlike Chandler's man of honor) but with removing Merle's fear of men so that she would be open to sexual conquest. (*Raymond Chandler on Screen*)

Credits

Producer	Robert Brassler
Director	John Brahm
Screenplay	Dorothy Hannah
Adaptation	Leonard Praskins
Director of Photography	Lloyd Ahern
Special Effects	Fred Sersen
Art Directors	James Basevi & Richard Irvine
Music	David Buttolph

Music Director	Alfred Newman
Editor	Harry Reynolds

Cast

Philip Marlowe	George Montgomery
Merle Davis	Nancy Guild
Leslie Murdock	Conrad Janis
Lieut. Breeze	Roy Roberts
Vannier	Fritz Kortner
Mrs. Murdock	Florence Bates
Blair	Marvin Miller
Morningstar	Houseley Stevenson
Sergeant Spangler	Bob Adler
George Anson	Jack Conrad
Eddie Prue	Alfred Linder

MARLOWE. Katzka-Berne Productions, Inc. and Cherokee Productions. A joint venture in association with Beckerman Productions, Inc. Presented by Metro-Goldwyn-Mayer, 1969. 95 min. sd., Metrocolor, 35 mm. Rated M. Adapted from *The Little Sister*.

With the Fifties and early Sixties dominated by the likes of KISS ME DEADLY and GUNN, Marlowe did not reappear as a film character until 1969, nearly twenty-five years after THE BRASHER DOUBLOON. In adapting *The Little Sister*, it was necessary to update a topical 1949 popular literary work into a relevant film experience, as well as transpose Marlowe from the studio nightworld of the fearful Forties into the on-location, shining-color and flashing freeway Los Angeles of the Sixties. ("Raymond Chandler and the World You Live IN")

Examples of this modernization was Marlowe's increased sexual activities and the introduction of smartly dressed, foot-kicking Winslow-Wong (played by Bruce Lee) in place of several of Chandler's minor characters. Another example of this update was the introduction of a theme song, a "first" for a Marlowe picture. The theme "Little Sister" was utilized throughout the film. The critical reactions to MARLOWE and Garner's portrayal of Marlowe was mixed; one critic labled the film "the most promising sleeper of 1946." Still, MARLOWE did reflect the mood of *The Little Sister* and remained faithful to the novel in terms of Marlowe's character.

Credits

Producers	Gabriel Katzka & Sidney Beckerman
Director	Paul Bogart
Screenplay	Sterling Silliphant
Director of Photography	William H. Daniels
Art Directors	George W. Davis & Addison Hehr
Music	Peter Matz
Song: "Little Sister"	
Words	Norman Gimbel
Music	Peter Matz
Recording Artist	Orpheus
Editor	Gene Ruggiero

Cast

Philip Marlowe	James Garner

Mavis Wald	Gayle Hunnicutt
Lt. Christy French	Carroll O'Connor
Dolores Gonzales	Rita Moreno
Orfamay Quest	Sharon Ferrell
Mr. Crowell	William Daniels
Sonny Steelgrave	H. M. Wynant
Grant Hicks	Jackie Coogan
Julie	Corrinne Camacho
Winslow Wong	Bruce Lee
Dr. Vincent Lagardie	Paul Stevens
Orrin Quest	Roger Newman

THE LONG GOODBYE. United Artists, 1973. Camera and lenses by Panavision, 112 min., sd., color. Rated R. Based on the novel by Raymond Chandler.

    THE LONG GOODBYE was not released as a film (March 1973) until nearly twenty years after the novel was published. Director Robert Altman and screenwriter Leigh Brackett did not attempt to modernize Marlowe. In fact, they commented that Philip Marlowe would be pathetically out of place in the Seventies, and that THE LONG GOODBYE would put him out of his misery. Altman even claimed to have killed off Marlowe by "using up" Chandler's last novel. (*Raymond Chandler on Screen*)

    THE LONG GOODBYE presented Marlowe as an anachronism, ill-equipped to function in the absurdist world around him. Elliot Gould portrayed a passive Marlowe; he wandered in a daze, as though not quite awake. Gould drifted through events without contributing or reacting. Contrary to Chandler's Marlowe, Gould did not represent a catalyst; he portrayed a born loser who did not have self-assurance, loyalty, or honor.

    As can be expected, many critics were offended to see Marlowe presented as a zonked-out loser. Others, however, praised the film especially for its satire and humor. It is safe to comment that Altman's offbeat and irreverent adaptation of *The Long Goodbye* was one of the more controversial films of the Seventies.

Credits

Executive Producer	Elliot Kastner
Producer	Jerry Bick
Director	Robert Altman
Screenplay	Leigh Brackett
Director of Photography	Vilmostz Sigmond
Sound	John V. Speak
Music	John Williams
Title Song: Lyrics	Johnny Mercer
Music	John Williams
Editor	Lou Lombardo

Cast

Philip Marlowe	Elliot Gould
Eileen Wade	Nina Van Pallandt
Roger Wade	Sterling Hayden
Marty Augustine	Mark Rydell
Dr. Verringer	Henry Gibson
Harry	David Arkin

Lonnie Morgan	Warren Berlinger
Jo Ann Eggenweiler	Jo An Brody
Detective Farmer	Steve Coit
Detective Green	Jerry Jones
Detective Dayton	Tracy Harris
Pepe	Pepe Callahan

FAREWELL, MY LOVELY. Elliot Kastner/Independent Television Corp., 1975. Released by Avco Embassy. 97 min., sd., Fujicolor. Rated R. Based on the novel by Raymon Chandler.

The third and most recent adaptation of the novel *Farewell, My Lovely* is a study in contrasts, both as an R-rated version of Chandler's Los Angeles and as a showcase for Robert Mitchum's portrayal of Philip Marlowe. Contrary to a statement found in Stephen Pendo's *Raymond Chandler on Screen*, Mitchum played a cynical detective in the film OUT OF THE PAST (1947). This role foreshadowed his portrayal of Marlowe by nearly thirty years.

FAREWELL, MY LOVELY was produced as a period piece and set in Los Angeles of 1941. As a result, this adaptation is the only Marlowe film not set in the era during which it was produced. Director Dick Richards concentrated on recreating Chandler's milieu more so than examining the Marlowe/private eye stereotype. According to Richards, "[We] had to get the real smell of the Los Angeles of the period . . . and the real sounds, too. . . . And the real language. Chandler wrote dialogue the way people really spoke. . . . [He] wrote what critics call the classic detective story. We . . . tried to be faithful to his legacy and his style by creating the basic classic detective movie." (*Raymond Chandler on Screen*)

The plot of FAREWELL, MY LOVELY was generally faithful to the novel. One noticeable exception is Marlowe's increased involvement with violence and death--Marlowe kills three people in self defense including a woman (Velma). Premiering on August 13, 1975, FAREWELL, MY LOVELY was well received by the public and critics. Rex Reed remarked that "it was the kind of movie Bogart would have stood in line to see."

Credits

Executive Producers	Elliot Kastner & Jerry Bick
Producers	George Pappas & Jerry Bruckheimer
Director	Dick Richards
Screenplay	David Zelag Goodman
Director of Photography	John Alonzo
Art Director	Angelo Graham
Music	David Shire
Editors	Walter Thompson & Joel Cox

Cast

Philip Marlowe	Robert Mitchum
Mrs. Grayle (Velma)	Charlotte Rampling
Lieut. Nulty	John Ireland
Mrs. Jesse Florian	Sylvia Miles
Moose Malloy	Jack O'Halloran

Larry Brunette	Anthony Zerbe
Detective Billy Rolfe	Harry Dean Stanton
Mr. Grayle	Jim Thompson
Marriott	John O'Leary
Francis Amthor	Kate Murtagh
Tommy Ray	Walter McGinn
Jonnie	Sylvester Stallone
Georgie	Jimmy Archer

SOURCES

American Film Institute. "Whodunit? Fifty Tales of Mayhem, Murder and Menace Featuring the Greatest Detectives." AFI Theater Program Brochure, 5 Jan-12 Feb 1977.

Baxter, John. *The Gangster Film*. New York: Barnes, 1970.

Cohen, Mitchell. "Film Noir: Villains and Victims." *Film Comment* 10 (Nov-Dec 1974).

Durham, Philip. *Down These Streets a Man Must Go: Raymond Chandler's Knight*. Chapel Hill: UNC Press, 1963.

Everson, William. *The Detective in Film*. Secaucus: Citadel, 1972.

Gabree, John. *Gangsters: From Little Caesar to the Godfather*. New York: Galahad, 1973.

Hagen, Ordean. *Who Done It? A Guide to Detective, Mystery and Suspense Fiction*. New York: Bowker, 1969.

Jameson, Richard. "Film Noir: Raymond Chandler and the World You Live In." *Film Comment* 10 (Nov-Dec 1974).

MacShane, Frank. *The Life of Raymond Chandler*. New York: Dutton, 1976.

_____. "Raymond Chandler and Hollywood." *American Film* 1 (April-May 1976).

Michael, Paul, ed. *The American Movies Reference Book: The Sound Era*. New York: Prentice Hall, 1972.

The New York Times Film Reviews 1912-1968. Vols. III & IV, 1939-1948, 1949-1959. New York: Arno Press, 1970.

Parish, James, ed. *The Great Movie Series*. New York: Barnes, 1971.

Pendo, Stephen. *Raymond Chandler on Screen: His Novels into Film*. Metuchen: Scarecrow, 1976.

Steinbrunner, Chris, & Otto Penzler, eds. *The Encyclopedia of Mystery and Detection*. New York: McGraw-Hill, 1976.

THE DEGENERATION OF DONALD HAMILTON
By George Kelley

Once upon a time, Donald Hamilton wrote a minor classic. Its title is *Line of Fire* (Dell, 1955; other editions by Fawcett). It was superior to the first, and best, of the famous Matt Helm series, *Death of a Citizen*.

The latest in the Helm series is on the news stands, *The Terrorizers* (Fawcett, 1977). It is a bad book.

In 22 years, from *Line of Fire* to the tacky *Terrorizers*, something happened to Donald Hamilton. In 22 years, Hamilton degenerated from a promising writer to an author whose work in recent years is embarrassing to read. What happened?

Let's look at Hamilton's minor classic first.

Line of Fire is an original. I've never read anything like it. The narrator and hero, Paul Nyquist, has a secret that completely dominates his life. He is impotent.

During a hunting trip, Nyquist saves a hunter from death by killing a wild boar. The hunter is gangster Carl Gunderman. Gunderman panicked when the boar charged; Nyquist is the only man alive who knows Gunderman is a coward. Yet, before the boar dies, Nyquist is injured, rendered impotent.

A strange relationship develops between the two men. Each knows the other's awful secret. Gunderman rewards Nyquist by setting him up in a gun shop. Nyquist takes on two partners and the shop is known throughout the country for its fine work.

But Nyquist is still manipulated by Gunderman's knowledge. Gunderman controls the Governor, and the Governor is facing a tough election ahead for Senator. Too many people suspect links between Governor Maney and the criminal element, that is, Gunderman.

In order to sever that line of thought, Gunderman has Nyquist, a weapons expert and marksman, attempt an assassination of the Governor. But this is an assassination with a difference: Nyquist is supposed to *miss* the Governor, but make it look good for the press.

Unfortunately for the Governor, he throws up his arm just as Nyquist pulls the trigger and BANG! goodby Governor Maney's arm.

The plot unravels, but the suspense is always there. And the writing has a hard, gritty style:

> Neither of us had really been much good, to ourselves or anybody else. Well, no reason to leave the job half done. I walked over to the rack of guns on the wall, took down the .45 automatic, and decided it was too much gun for the job. No sense in making that much of a mess for somebody to clean up.
>
> I put it back and got the target .22. I took a loaded clip from the drawer, shoved it into place, and jacked up a shell. Then I stuck the barrel into my mouth, and waited to see what I was made of.

The writing is flat, but the power lurks there, you can feel it.

Line of Fire is a very good book, Hamilton's best.

But *The Terrorizers* is another matter entirely.

Over the life of the Matt Helm series, the major character has slowly lost credibility and gained bad habits. Chiefly, Helm talks too much. He pontificates. (Perhaps this is an occupational hazard that afflicts all aging superspies; Altee's Joe Gall fell prey to the same sort of non-stop dialogue.)

When there is action, Helm handles it effortlessly. There is no suspense here, no urgency. We all know that Matt Helm will triumph.

The gritty, powerful writing is gone. In its place is dull prose. The characters are cardboard. The plot is most embarrassing: Helm has amnesia after crashing into the sea. He is told in the hospital that he is a photographer named Paul Madden, but the phone rings and the voice on the other end tells him that he's Helm.

But the amnesia ploy is never really used, other than a temporary refuge from some torture. Helm, without memory, acts suspiciously like Helm with his memory.

The rest of the plot involves the Mafia and some terrorists who are setting off bombs. It really doesn't make a great deal of sense.

Finally, we have the character of Helm; once, in *Death of a Citizen*, Helm was a cynical, war-weary, retired spy reactivated because of necessity. The violence in the book was brutal, but understated.

In *The Terrorizers*, violence is a joke, and so is Helm himself:

> They pumped a lot of corpuscles into me and dug a lot of lead out. The final tally was one 9mm submachinegun bullet, two .38-caliber pistol bullets, and two little round Number One Buckshot balls. The last two hadn't done much damage.

Writing something like that does do a lot of damage: to your character's realism and to your own reputation as a writer. Superman was created in the 1930's and Matt Helm is a damn poor stand-in. He couldn't even make it as The Bionic Man.

Once, 22 years ago, Donald Hamilton wrote a book worth reading and rereading; in 1977, Hamilton produced a comic book without pictures that isn't worth your time.

THE MYSTERIOUS JOHN DICKSON CARR
By Larry L. French

It has been noted that John "Dickson" Carr wrote at least a couple of "pulp" stories, one of which having appeared in the May 1935 *Dime Mystery Magazine* under the byline of John "Dixon" Carr. R. E. Briney has indicated that the misspelled middle name left the true authorship in doubt until 1970 when Carr, himself, confirmed responsibility for the story. But was "Dixon" misspelled?

John Dickson Carr died on February 27, 1977, but how old was he? His obituary in the Greenville, South Carolina *News* dated March 1, 1977, indicated that he was born in 1905 in Uniontown, Pa. A "Profile" authored by Robert Lewis Taylor in *The New Yorker* magazine (1951) says 1906. *Time* magazine, in its "Milestones" section of March 14, 1977, indicates that at the time of his death Mr. Carr was seventy years of age. The 1942 *Twentieth Century Authors* by Kunitz and Haycraft indicates a birth year of 1905, but *Contemporary Authors* notes 1906 (CA also listed "John Rhode" as another pseudonym of Carr which obviously is inaccurate; John Rhode and Carter Dickson, the true pseudonym of Carr, co-authored *Fatal Descent* in 1939).

According to R. E. Briney, in his "Tribute to JDC" (TAD 10/2), John Dickson Carr was born on November 30, 1906, which, indeed, would have made him seventy at the time of his death. In a communication from his estate's legal representative, however, the "Grand Master of Mystery" is referred to as "John *Dixon* Carr".

The fact that additional "stories" written by JDC keep turning up is not surprising. I, myself, recently uncovered an article written for *Harper's* in January 1941 entitled, "When Conan Doyle Was Sherlock Holmes". In addition to the Taylor "Profile", I find (so far) only one other extensive article of Mr. Ca·r, that being written by Roger Herzel and incorporated as a chapter in Hoyt's *Minor American Novelists* (S.I.U. Press, 1971).

Indeed, John Dickson Carr was a very private man and was actually publicity shy. He kept no manuscripts. He wrote by sitting behind the typewriter and typing out an exact copy and if a mistake was made, that particular page was torn up (or corrected) and thrown away. All manuscripts came out letter-perfect and no drafts were ever made or left over.

Mr. Carr and his family moved frequently, and during the course of such transit, all papers, books (Taylor, in his article, noted that JDC had, at one time, perhaps the finest crime book collection in the world, which included the top secret *English Coroner's Official Handbook of Poisons*) and artifacts. The only papers remaining are those of a financial nature and it is reported that Mrs. Carr has only one letter in her possession with John Dickson Carr's signature. It would be interesting to review this document in regard to the spelling of "Dickson".

Another JDC "mystery" centers around the Conan Doyle authorization for Carr's biography of Sir Arthur. Taylor's version is that Carr and Adrian Doyle had become fast friends in 1941 and, being displeased with the Pearson version, Adrian specifically pleaded with Carr to do the biography. Michael Harrison (noted Sherlockian and author) disagrees and tells us that JDC voluntarily commenced research on the man wh he admired so, and Adrian rose up to threaten all sorts of things and announced that Carr had not been authorized to write about Sir Arthur (as if anyone needs anyone's authorization to write about anyone else). Matters were patched up, however, and JDC wrote the biography with Adrian's "collaboration". The article referred to herein (*Harper's*, January 1949) was billed as "an article which will later form a chapter" in the Conan Doyle biography. The book appeared the same year (1949) as the article, again another "mystery".

John Dickson Carr is clearly recognized as the "Master of the Locked-Room Mystery". Taylor describes Carr as working in a "locked-room", "ascending to the attic around 8 a.m., occasionally kicking out at dark corners en route to be sure they are not tenanted with the sort of citizenry he habitually creates. In practically all respects, his chamber is conducive to the germination of macabre prose." Clearly, John Dickson Carr lived as he wrote . . . in a very mysterious and perhaps bizarre manner.

FOR SALE: Crime/Mystery Fiction. All wants searched free of charge. Try me!   S. B. Johns
                 12 Forest View
                 Neath, S. Wales
                 GREAT BRITAIN

Many SAINT, MANHUNT, EQMM from '50s. One dollar each. No large size MANHUNTS. Add 35¢ postage per order. Many '40s EQMM at $2 each.   Jonathan White
                 286 Corbin Place, 6B
                 Brooklyn, NY 11235

THE NERO WOLFE SAGA
Part IV
By Guy M. Townsend

In the Best Families [April-September 1950], published in 1950. WARNING--Important plot developments are discussed in this section, though the murderer's identity is not revealed.

THE STORY ::: This is without doubt the most unusual episode of the entire Wolfe Saga. Wealthy Mrs. Barry Rackham hires Wolfe to find out where her husband, who has no money of his own, has been getting the considerable sums he has been spending. Archie visits the Rackham country estate on a pretext but before he can learn anything Mrs. Rackham is discovered stabbed to death. This much of the tale, together with the eventual explanation of who done it and how, would have made an excellent short story. What promotes *In the Best Families* into the novel class is the Zeck element. It is evident almost from the beginning that Rackham is Zeck's man, and a booby-trapped package, which could have been a bomb but was only tear gas, makes it clear that Zeck wants Wolfe off the case. Then Zeck calls and tells Wolfe to lay off, offering to pay him the $10,000 fee which Mrs. Rackham has put up if he will abandon the case. Naturally, Wolfe refuses to be intimidated and Archie goes out to the Rackham country place where Mrs. Rackham is then murdered. Archie immediately phones Wolfe with this news and when he returns to the brownstone the next day he finds the front door open and Wolfe gone. Wolfe has left him a terse note, which reads in full: "AG: Do not look for me. My very best regards and wishes. NW." What has happened is obvious. Wolfe has decided that the time for a showdown with Zeck has arrived and has gone to ground to prepare himself. But his departure is not quite according to plan; Archie remembers Wolfe's earlier remark that, should the necessity of fighting Zeck arise, "I shall move to a base of operations which will be known only to Mr. Goodwin and perhaps two others," and he is thoroughly miffed that Wolfe has neglected to keep him informed. (Archie says: "Certainly the two others he had had in mind were Saul Panzer and Marko Vukcic.") Archie receives indirect communications from Wolfe from two sources. The first is an ad which Wolfe puts in the *Gazette*:

MR. NERO WOLFE
ANNOUNCES HIS RETIREMENT
FROM THE DETECTIVE BUSINESS
TODAY, APRIL 10, 1950

Mr. Wolfe will not hereafter be available. Inquiries from clients on unfinished matters may be made of Mr. Archie Goodwin. Inquiries from others that clients will not receive attention.

Archie interprets this as Wolfe's way of telling him to

lay off the Rackham case, since Mrs. Rackham was the client and she is dead. The other comes from Marko, with whom Wolfe spoke briefly before disappearing. Marko tells him that Wolfe has arranged for Hewitt to move the plants to his place; that Fritz is to come to work at Rusterman's; that Marko is to have a power of attorney; that Marko is "to offer the house and its contents for sale"; and that Wolfe's specific instructions for Archie are that "You are to act in the light of experience as guided by intelligence." A big help, that. Archie's big problem is that "it was not inconceivable that Wolfe had decided to chuck it for good," and his own position was accordingly up in the air. It becomes clear after a while that Wolfe is remaining in touch, at least occasionally, with Marko, because Marko has Archie bring him at different times two checks for $5,000 made out to cash.

When a month goes by with no word from Wolfe, Archie decides to strike out on his own and goes into business for himself. He rents a small office "on Madison Avenue, tenth floor, in the forties", room number 1019, buys himself some good used office furniture (not taking anything from the brownstone), and opens for business as "ARCHIE GOODWIN, Private Detective". "I was not kidding myself that I had really cut loose, since I hadn't moved my bed out [of the brownstone], but the way I figured it a caretaker who is drawing no pay [Archie stopped his pay check when he opened his own office] has a right to a room; and besides, Fritz was still sleeping there and we were splitting on the groceries for breakfast, and I didn't want to insult either him or my stomach by breaking that up."

Archie does pretty well on his own--"My idea was to net more per week than I had been getting from Wolfe, not that I cared for the money, but as a matter of principle." We know, from a remark he makes elsewhere in this tale, that Wolfe was paying him $1,000 per month, so let's see how he does. In his first month, May, he is just getting set up and getting the word spread around that he's in business, so he only nets $415 above expenses, but from then on he hits his stride. In June he nets $1270 and in July he gets up to about $4,000, and by August he is thinking about taking a vacation in Norway with Lily Rowan. "Slow but sure, I was working around to an attitude toward life without Nero Wolfe on a permanent basis."

Finally, on 22 August, four days before his land Lily's ship was to sail from New York, Archie is approached by a mysterious gangster named Pete Roeder--"He was no one I had ever seen or heard of. . . . This bird was a complete stranger. With more skin supplied for his face than was needed, it had taken up the slack in pleats and wrinkles, and that may have accounted for his sporting a pointed brown beard, since it must be hard to shave pleats." He also talks through his nose. Archie doesn't recognize him at all, but all you smart cookies out there have already guessed that it's good old Nero Wolfe himself. Before Wolfe reveals himself, Archie is so indiscreet as to make the following remark to "Roeder": "I freely admit he [Wolfe] had his good points. I have often mentioned them and appreciated them, but as the months go by one fact about him stands out clearer than anything else. He was a pain in the ass." Ahem! Archie tries to pretend he knew it all the time, but Wolfe will have none of that--"Pfui. You hadn't the slightest inkling." Wolfe says he has lost 117 pounds and that he, "Roeder", looks "like a sixteenth-century prince of Savoy named Philibert." Archie immediately begins to berate Wolfe for not letting him know anything and Wolfe says, "I expected this, of course. It is you, and since I decided long ago to put up with you, I even welcome it. But you, also long ago, decided to put up with me. Are we going to shake hands or not?" They do.

Wolfe fills Archie in on what has happened since he decamped. He went from New York to Texas, where he lost the weight and began the beard. From there he went to Los Angeles, where he built up his reputation as a disreputable but brilliant character, devising a scheme "for getting considerable sums of money from ten different people simultaneously, with a minimum of risk." His success enabled him to come back to New York (on 12 July) and sign on with Zeck as a "D" in Zeck's criminal hierarchy. Wolfe realizes that he is in a life and death struggle with Zeck, and that only one of them will come through it alive, and his plans have reached the point where he needs Archie's assistance. To enable them to communicate at length without arousing the suspicion of Zeck or any of his henchmen, Lily Rowan is roped into the deal to pose as Roeder's "woman." Lily shrewdly realizes Roeder's true identity, but plays along splendidly, necking madly with old Pete in the back seat while Zeck's man drives the car.

Archie gets "drafted" by Zeck's organization to assist "Roeder" and is put on the "B" list. He finally gets to meet Zeck face to face in the latter's secret lair: "There was nothing to him but his forehead and eyes. It wasn't a forehead, it was a dome, sloping up and up to the line of his faded thin hair. The eyes were the result of an error on the assembly line. They had been intended for a shark and someone got careless. They did not now look the same as shark eyes because Arnold Zeck's brain had been using them to see with for fifty years, and that had had an effect." "He blinked perhaps one-tenth his share." And Archie speaks of "his hard, cold, precise voice that never went up or down." During the course of Zeck's first interview with Archie, the former remarks, with "Roeder" present: "There was one man who matched me in intellect-- the man you worked for, Nero Wolfe--but his will failed him. His vanity wouldn't let him yield, and he cleared out." But Zeck is not allowed to harbor that illusion for much longer, and he learns Roeder's true identity just seconds before his own ingeniously arranged murder takes place. With Zeck dead, his criminal empire quickly crumbles and Wolfe sheds his Roeder guise and returns to the brownstone, where he resumes his old habits and gains a full ten pounds in three days flat. There remains only the clearing up of the murder of Mrs. Rackham, which Wolfe accomplishes with a splendid and lucid explanation of who done it and how, which had this reader kicking himself for not having figured it out himself.

WOLFE ::: Most of the information regarding Wolfe has

already been touched on in the preceeding discussion, but there are a few items left to mention. His house in Egypt is again spoken of, as a possible place where he might be hiding out; his age is given as "around fifty"; and Wolfe never wore a watch until he strapped one on his wrist as a part of his Roeder disguise. Presumably he abandoned it with the beard. Lastly, Archie muses on an aspect of Wolfe's reaction to women: "I have never figured out Wolfe's grounds for deciding whether or not to get to his feet when a woman enters his office. If they're objective they're too complicated for me, and if they're subjective I wouldn't know where to start."

ARCHIE ::: Archie calls himself "Wolfe's secretary, trusted assistant and official gnat." He appears to have aged slightly since his age was last mentioned, since he refers to a 34 year old man as being about his own age. "I'm fairly good with a billiard cue," Archie tells us, "and only Saul Panzer can beat me at tailing a man or woman in New York, but what I am best at is reporting a complicated event to Nero Wolfe." Somewhat surprisingly, he uses the words "trepidant vigilance." Wolfe bestows another "satisfactory" on him, though in this instance no special significance is attached to it. Archie spends twenty hours in the Westchester slammer as a material witness because the Westchester boys won't believe that he doesn't know Wolfe's whereabouts, and he is eventually sprung by Nathaniel Parker. While Wolfe is away, Archie receives several offers of employment from the FBI, all of which he refuses. Archie's $1,000 per month salary has already been mentioned, and the following exchange takes place when Archie and Wolfe meet again after Wolfe's long absence--Archie: "I've been taking it easy, so my income from detective work has only been a little more than double what you were paying me." Wolfe" "I don't believe it."

OTHER REGULARS """ "Nathaniel Parker, the only lawyer Wolfe has ever been willing to invite to dinner," makes only a brief appearance, while Lily Rowan, as has been described, has her biggest role since *Some Buried Caesar*. Theodore appears briefly; when Wolfe goes to ground he arranges for Hewitt to take Theodore on at $200 a week, so odds are Wolfe has been paying him about half that. Incidentally, Archie doesn't like him: "Look Theodore. . . . I don't give a good goddam what you like or don't like. Mr. Wolfe has always pampered you because you're the best orchid nurse alive. This is as good a time as any to tell you that you remind me of sour milk." Wolfe also arranges a job for Fritz at Marko's restaurant, Rusterman's. Wolfe suggests that Marko should pay him $2,000 per month, but Marko only pays him $1,500. Wolfe, however, was only paying him $1,000 per month, the same as he paid Archie. Marko, of course, has an important if minor role. Archie says he "was the only man in New York who called Wolfe by his first name." Lon Cohen is mentioned, and Saul, Fred and Orrie do some work for Archie: "Saul was undersized, inconspicuous all but his nose, and the best a-l-round man alive. Fred Durkin was big and clumsy, with a big red face, with no Doberman pinscher in him but plenty of bulldog. Orrie Cather was slender and muscular and handsome, just the man to mingle with the guests at a swell dinner party when circumstances called for it." (Note that Orrie's description has changed somewhat from earlier episodes.) In another place Archie says "Saul Panzer is the best man alive. Cather and Durkin are way above average." Saul's wife and children are mentioned again. There is one discordant note here. Fred Durkin, whose phenomenal tailing ability has been commented on by Archie, is said by Archie to have unintentionally allowed himself to be spotted at least three times on a tail in a single day. This simply cannot be reconciled with Fred's admitted, though unexpected, ability.

The Westchester gang comes in for some more descriptions. There is "my pet Westchester hate, Lieutenant Con Noonan," about whom Archie at one point remarks: "No doubt life was hard for him--born with the instincts of a Hitler or Stalin in a country where people are determined to do their own voting." Archie also says "he has the meanest smile I know of except maybe Boris Karloff." Ben Dykes, "the dean of the Westchester County dicks," puts in an appearance, as does Westchester County District Attorney Cleveland Archer, who was "slightly plumper than he had been a year ago." And the boys in the NYPD also have parts of varying importance to play. Lieutenant Rowcliff, "the Con Noonan of the New York Police Department," is just mentioned, and "one evening I [Archie] ran into Sergeant Purley Stebbins at Jake's and bought him a lobster," during the consumption of which Purley was persuaded to part with some information regarding the status of the investigation of Mrs. Rackham's murder. This is the first mention, by the way, of "Jake's". And then there is Inspector Cramer--"a chunky specimen about my height, with wrinkled pink skin and gray hair and sharp gray-blue eyes." He calls Archie by his first name again: "Over the years he had called me Archie only when he wanted something awful bad or when he had something wrapped up that Wolfe had given him and his humanity overcame him." This time, however, he has dropped by to ask Archie where Wolfe is. When Archie denies being privy to the where and why of Wolfe's departure, Cramer shrewdly guesses that Wolfe has gone to earth to get Zeck. He then tells Archie to tell Wolfe to come back, give up on the Rackham case, and leave Zeck alone: "I want you to understand, Archie, why I came here. Wolfe is too cocky to live. He has enough brass and bluster to outfit a thousand sergeants. Sure, I know him; I ought to. I would love to bloody his nose for him, I've tried to often enough, and some day I will and enjoy it. But I would hate to seem him break his neck on a deal like this where he hasn't got a chance." Archie makes Cramer so angry by suggesting that he might be speaking for Zeck that the Inspector throws a couple of punches at him (without connecting) then storms out of the brownstone. Before leaving Cramer we should mention his salary and his cigar. About the first, Cramer says he makes about ten thousand a year. About the second, Archie remarks, "Cramer moved the cigar--getting shorter now, although he never lit one--to the other side of his mouth."

PHYSICAL ASPECTS ::: No address for the brownstone

this time, but the following remark by Archie pins it down pretty closely: "I went on across Tenth Avenue, on nearly to Eleventh, and pulled up to the curb in front of Wolfe's old brownstone house." We are told (for the first time?) that Fritz's room is in the basement, and we learn a bit more about some items in the office. For example, Wolfe keeps a gold bottle opener in his desk drawer, a gift from a happy client. And Archie supplies us with some specifics regarding his arsenal--"I opened a desk drawer and got out the Grisson .38. My favorite Colt, taken from me in Zeck's antechamber, was gone forever." We are told, for the first time, that there is a "table over by the big globe," and the one way glass panel in the front door is mentioned again. Finally, during Wolfe's absence Archie "put one of the cars, the big sedan, in dead storage." Oh, yes, two more items: we are told that Lily Rowan lives in a "penthouse apartment on East Sixty-third Street," and we learn that Rusterman's Restaurant, "the only place where Wolfe really liked to eat except at home," is on 54th St. (Marko lives on the third floor.)

ROUTINE AT THE BROWNSTONE ::: In this markedly *un*-routine novel there are only two items for this section. "He [Wolfe] pressed the button twice--the beer signal." Can this really be the first time the beer signal has been identified? Or the first time that "the button" has been mentioned? I'm falling down on my job disgracefully. The other item is really a break with routine: "I became aware that I was sitting in Wolfe's chair behind his desk. That brought me up with a jerk. No one else, including me, ever sat in that chair, but there I was. I didn't approve of it. It seemed to imply that Wolfe was through with that chair for good, and that was a hell of an attitude to take, no matter how sore I was."

ODDS AND ENDS ::: Reference is made to two non-canonical cases--"A case which I will not identify by name because it was never allowed to get within a mile of a newspaper or a microphone," and "a poison-letter job that was the main item of unfinished business" at the time of Wolfe's hasty departure, and which Archie and Fred finish up in Wolfe's absence. The first mention ever of poker is made in this episode--Archie, Saul, Fred, Orrie and Fritz play at the brownstone. Archie loses $12.00 and "Saul was the big winner." Archie eats at Mart's Diner on 11th Ave., apparently not for the first time since he and Mart seem to be acquainted. (It is not clear whether Mart is a he or a she.) Zeck's country estate is called Eastcrest. The Great Orchid Massacre is referred to several times. In one instance Archie says the damage came to $38,000 [not $40,000], and in another he speaks of the Massacre "ruining ten thousand dollars' worth of glass and equipment and turning eight thousand valuable orchid plants into a good start on a compost heap." Which brings up an interesting question--are Wolfe's orchid plants only worth a little more than three bucks apiece? In addition to the two $5,000 checks he has Marko cash for him, Wolfe also took $3,000 cash from the safe when he left the brownstone. It does not appear that he touched the $50,000 stashed in the New Jersey safe deposit box, since he asks Archie if he had occasion to make use of those funds. So apparently the $50,000 is still there. It will be interesting to see if any further mention is made of it later on in the Saga [I don't recall any].

Lastly, Archie gets to take his one-month vacation to Norway with Lily, and while there he receives a letter from Wolfe. The treatment of this episode is already so ridiculously long that I don't see how another long quote can make things much worse, so I'll close this chapter by quoting the letter in full:

Dear Archie:

The chickens came from Mr. Haskins Friday, four of them, and they were satisfactory. Marko came to dinner. He misses Fritz, he says. I have given Fritz a raise.

Mr. Cramer dropped in for a talk one day last week. He made some rather pointed comments about you, but on the whole behaved himself tolerably.

I am writing this longhand because I do not like the way the man sent by the agency types.

Vanda peetersiana has a raceme 29 in. long. Its longest last year was 22 in. We have found three snails in the warm room. I thought of mailing them to Mr. Hewitt but didn't.

[The murderer] hanged himself in the jail at White Plains yesterday and was dead when discovered. That of course cancels your promise to Mr. Archer to return in time for the trial, but I trust you will not use it as an excuse to prolong your stay.

We have received your letters and they were most welcome. I have received an offer of $315 for the furniture in your office but am insisting on $350. Fritz says he has written you. I am beginning to feel more like myself.

My best regards,
NW

"Disguise for Murder" [March 1950], published in *Curtains for Three*, 1950. [Baring-Gould, blast him, dates this one *before* the just discussed novel, but places it *after* it in the chronology, a fact which I have just now noticed as I type this stencil. Damn it to hell.]

THE STORY ::: Quite uncharacteristically, Wolfe lets Bill McNab, garden editor at the *Gazette*, talk him into holding an open house for members of the Manhattan Flower Club. Some 219 members and their guests arrive and mill around the brownstone, mostly in the plant rooms, from 2:30 until 5:30 in the afternoon. Saul and Fritz do the honors at the door, checking guests in and out, while Wolfe, Archie and Theodore remain accessible in the plant rooms. During this gathering a young woman is murdered in Wolfe's office, shortly after telling Archie that she has spotted a murderer among the guests. Unavoidably, the police are called in, and Rowcliff and Cramer gleefully grasp at this chance to annoy Wolfe and Archie. Rowcliff goes through both desks in the office on the pretext of examining the murder scene, and then Cramer spitefully orders the office sealed indefinitely. This intolerable situation provides Wolfe with the strongest motivation for solving the murder, which he does by shrewdly spotting the essential clue which can only point at one person (once a rather shakey assumption is made). But knowing who done it and proving it are two different things, and to secure proof Wolfe devises a stratagem which involves putting Archie in considerable danger, a circumstance to which Wolfe is not insensitive. The proof is obtained, and Archie gets shot in the shoulder in the process, in a splendidly surprising unmasking scene which takes place outside of the brownstone (and out of Wolfe's presence).

WOLFE ::: Only two items for this category this time around. Archie says that the chair at Wolfe's desk is "the only spot on earth where he was ever completely comfortable." And his finger gets another workout--"Wolfe sat with his eyes shut, but I got an idea of his state of mind from the fact that intermittently his forefinger was making little circles on the polished top of the table."

ARCHIE ::: This category isn't much better. Archie says "I've got a mother . . . and three aunts." Of his memory he says, "Whatever else my years as Wolfe's assistant may have done for me or to me, they have practically turned me into a tape recorder." His grammar slips at one point, when he says "it don't." And, he speaks of "my current and chronic campaign for a raise in wages," which is surprising because he has never before given any sign of being unhappy about his income.

OTHER REGULARS ::: Fritz's presence has already been mentioned, but it should also be pointed out that he displays an unexpected feistyness when he tackles a fellow who is trying to leave the brownstone before the police arrive. Theodore's presence in the plant rooms is merely noted, and Purley Stebbin's name is mentioned, but that's it for these two. Saul's presence on the scene has been mentioned. I was surprised to learn that Saul came *armed* to perform the presumably safe task of door-checking. Archie gives un another description of him: "Saul, only five feet seven, with the sharpest eyes and one of the biggest noses I have ever seen, in his unpressed brown suit, and his necktie crooked--he stood like Saul, not slouching and not stiff." When Cramer expresses skepticism at Saul's ability to remember the name of one of the 219 guests whom he had never seen before that day, Wolfe remarks to the inspector--"You should know by this time . . . that Mr. Panzer is an exceptional man." Cramer is more obnoxious than ever in this one, deliberately and unnecessarily sealing Wolfe's office for no other reason than to discommode his long-time rival. "This was far and away the worst Cramer had ever pulled. It was up to Wolfe. I looked at him. The blood had gone back down again; he was white with fury, and his mouth was pressed to so tight a line that there were no lips." Cramer says, "It's routine," whereupon "Wolfe's head came forward an inch, his chin out. 'No, Mr. Cramer. I'll tell you what it is. It is the malefic spite of a sullen little soul and a crabbed and envious mind. It is the childish rancor of a primacy too often challenged and offended. It is the feeble wiggle--'" Wolfe is interrupted at this point by the entrance of a witness. A pity, too, because he was just beginning to find his stride. Cramer's cigar is mentioned a couple of times. "Cramer got out a cigar, conveyed it to his mouth, and sank his teeth in it. He never lit one." "Cramer got out another cigar and rolled it between his palms, which was wasted energy since he didn't intend to draw smoke through it. Having seen him do it before, I knew what it meant. He still thought he might get something from this customer and was taking time out to control himself." Archie also has a few words to say about Lieutenant Rowcliff--"There were some city employees I liked, some I admired, some I had no feelings about, some I could have done without easy--and one whose ears I was going to twist someday. That was Rowcliff. He was tall, strong, handsome, and a pain in the neck." Two other cops are just mentioned--Levy and Murphy--probably for the only time, and an old acquaintance is mentioned--Dazy Perrit. Lastly, Doc Vollmer, whose house is said to be 200 yards down the street, and who "was taking on weight", is called in to confirm that the murder victim has indeed achieved corpsehood.

PHYSICAL ASPECTS ::: The one-way panel in the front door is still in use, and we learn for the first time that there are sever steps in the front stoop. The warm, moderate and cool rooms on the roof are mentioned, but most of the physical information in this episode relates to the office. This room, we are told for the first time, is "soundproofed, including the doors." There is a "cupboard" in the office in which the booze is kept. Countless drinks have been served in the office in earlier episodes, so there has doubtless been an earlier mention of the cupboard, but I must have missed it (them). The TV set in the office is mentioned again, as is Wolfe's gold bottle opener. The globe, too, is mentioned, but appears to have grown from two feet to three feet in diameter. (Actually, the size is mentioned by a guest, but neither Wolfe nor Archie contradicts it.)

ROUTINE AT THE BROWNSTONE ::: Is hopelessly disrupted in this one.

ODDS AND ENDS ::: When the police investigation keeps some of Wolfe's guests at the brownstone into dinner time, and when Cramer pulls his stunt of sealing the office, Wolfe has Fritz serve sandwiches to every one except the police. The sandwiches are sturgeon and ham--Georgia ham, Arhcie says to Cramer, rubbing it in, from "pigs fed on peanuts and acorns. Cured to Mr. Wolfe's specifications."

Murder by the Book [February-March 1951], published in 1951.

THE STORY ::: When Joan Wellman is killed the police dismiss it as a typical hit-and-run, but the girl's father, John Wellman from Peoria, Illinois, is convinced that it is murder and he hires Wolfe to find the killer. Joan was a manuscript reader for a publishing company and had a datt to meet "Baird Archer", a pseudonymous author whose novel she had rejected, on the night that she died. The name Baird Archer having been brought up by Inspector Cramer some weeks earlier in regard to the murder of a law clerk named Leonard Dykes, Wolfe is convinced that there must be a connection between the two deaths, and he and Archie set to work to discover the identity of this Baird Archer and to bring the murderer to justice. They succeed, of course, but not before the murderer claims a third victim, scarce minutes before Archie arrives on the scene.

WOLFE ::: There is a great deal about Wolfe in this one. His dislikes are particularly in evidence, beginning with his disliking for work (and his reasons for overcoming it):

> Wolfe hated to start his brain going on what he called work, and during the years I had been on his payroll the occasions had been rare when anything but a substantial retainer had jarred him into it. But he is not a loafer. He can't be, since his income as a private detective is what keeps that old house going, with the rooms full of orchid plants, with Theodore Horstmann as tender, and Fritz Brenner serving up the best meals in New York, and me, Archie Goodwin, asking for a raise every time I buy a new suit, and sometimes getting it. It takes a gross of at least ten thousand a month to get by.

Archie also tells us "Wolfe does not like conferences with clients. Many's the time he has told me not to let a client in." (Actually, this is the first mention Archie makes of this in the Saga.) Archie remarks on another of Wolfe's dislikes--again for the first time--"He hated the prospect of work during digestion," and Wolfe himself comments, "I dislike business with breakfast," though not before he has had a prolonged discussion of business over his breakfast tray with Archie. Wolfe's breakfast routine is again described: "Ordinarily Fritz takes Wolfe's breakfast tray up to him at eight o'clock," and there, dressed in the unvarying yellow pajamas, "sometimes Wolfe breakfasted in bed and sometimes at the table by the window." Besides disliking to discuss business at breakfast, "he never says a word if he can help it until his orange juice is down." Another of Wolfe's dislikes: "He always resented being interrupted in the middle of a London *Times* crossword puzzle." And here Archie mentions one we've encountered before: "Sometimes Wolfe makes an effort to conceal his dislike of shaking hands with strangers, and sometimes he doesn't." And Wolfe's greatest dislike--leaving the brownstone--is touched on several times, on one of which Archie says, "Wolfe never leaves the office on business, unless there is an incentive more urgent than the prospect of a fee, such as saving his own skin." In this case Archie flys to the west coast, at the thought of which Wolfe "shuddered. He regards a twenty-block taxi ride as a reckless gamble." His great relief at having Archie safely back again causes Wolfe--who remarks elsewhere in the story that "a schedule broken at will becomes a mere procession of vagaries"--to break with a firmly established routine. "Wolfe never came downstairs in the morning until after he finished in the plant rooms at eleven o'clock," but when Archie gets back from Los Angeles before that time he does just that. "He was actually breaking a rule. I thought it deserved some recognition and accepted his offer of a handshake." Wolfe says, "It is satisfactory to have you back." Wolfe's disliking for women comes to the surface in this episode when Archie proposes to have a dozen secretaries over to the brownstone for dinner (in the line of duty, of course). Wolfe flatly refuses, telling Archie to take them to Rusterman's instead. But after a moment's thought, in which Archie's determination to have the ladies over may have played a deciding role, Wolfe relents and agrees to let the ladies come, saying that he, Wolfe, would "dine with Marko, and spend the evening with him." Marko, incidentally, is referred to by Archie as Wolfe's "closest friend and owner of Rusterman's Restaurant." Further on the subject of women, Wolfe suggests to Crmaer that a female witness may be lying, and when Cramer asks, "What the hell for?" Wolfe replies, "Force of habit. The etiquette of the sex."

There is much more Wolfe lore still to be mentioned: Archie remarks on Wolfe's "seventh of a ton" and says that the chair behind his desk is "the only chair on earth that really suits him." Archie later remarks that "the kitchen is the only place on earth where he doesn't mind a chair that lets his fanny lap over the sides." Cramer makes the following remark to Wolfe: "One of the many reasons you're hard to take is that when you're being sarcastic you don't sound sarcastic. That's just one of your offensive habits." Another of Wolfe's habbits, this one a familiar one, is also mentioned: he "leaned back, closed his eyes, and started pushing his lips in and out, which meant he was working, and hard." And here's some further illumination on his beer drinking habits: "Wolfe, at his desk, was pouring beer. He put the bottle down, waited for the foam to subside to the right level so that the tilt would get him beer and would also moisten his lips with foam, lifted the glass, and drank. He liked to let the foam dry on his lips, but not when there was company, so he used his handkerchief before he spoke." At another place we are told, "Wolfe was indignant. To control his emotions, he closed his eyes and waggled his head." Wolfe's superb memory is in evidence in this episode, as is his laziness. Regarding the latter, Archie at one point inquires of Wolfe, "Sitzlust again?" [not sitzenlust, as he uses earlier in the Saga], and at another point Wolfe himself states: "You know quite well that for me pool is not play; it is exercise." In fact, however, Wolfe engages in some quite vigorous (for him) activities on this case: "Wolfe struck the arm of his chair with his palm, a gesture so violent with him that it was the next thing to hysterics"; and at another point Wolfe roars "Shut up!" Wolfe shows some signs of limbering up his vocabulary in this one: he speaks of the "Jackassery" of the police; to a lawyer he asks, "are you charging me with a malum? In se or Prohibitim?"; and he also uses "poopery", "pother" and "mendacity." The color of the smocks Wolfe wears in the plant rooms is mentioned for the first time. You guessed it, they're yellow. And while we're in the plant rooms we might also note Archie's comment that Wolfe is better at tying ribbons around boxes of flowers than either Theodore or Archie himself. Wolfe chuckles once in this one, and lastly, he is "reading a book of lyrics by Oscar Hammerstein."

ARCHIE ::: Wolfe's opinion of his assistant's abilities is high in this episode: "Mr. Goodwin may have his equal in making the acquaintance of a young woman and developing it into intimacy, but I doubt it"; and witness this: "It is always a pleasure to hear him say 'Satisfactory' when I have reported on an errand. This time he did better. . . . An emphatic 'Very satisfactory.'" But that doesn't keep Wolfe from shutting him out on one aspect of the case, which leads Archie to remark, "I always resent it when he sees fit to give one of the boys a chare that he thinks I don't need to know about." Archie's notebook is again in use, and we learn (how's this for useless knowledge?) that sauerkraut makes him belch--he lets us know that "eruct" is Latin for belch. When he has the secretaries over for dinner, "I took the chair at the head, Wolfe's place, the first time I had ever sat there," and afterwards he takes one of the secretaries dancing at the Bobolink, which is the first mention of this establishment. In fact, Archie does a lot of dancing in this one. As mentioned above, Archie goes to California in this episode, and, though there has been no mention of it in the Saga, it is clear that he has been there before on business: "I hadn't been to the west coast for several years"; while there he utilizes the services of the Southwest Agency in L.A., run by Ferdinand Dolman, saying that he had "been there once before, years back." Archie, by the way, has nothing good to say about California weather. Lastly, Archie, more in this episode than in any other to date (or perhaps later), is not above twisting things moderately to cover up his mistakes and hake himself look better.

OTHER REGULARS ::: Cramer, of course, is present, and even admits to wanting to "ask a little favor"; Archie says, "What was remarkable was his admitting it." Archie tells us that his face was "chronically red," which is not surprising considering his attitude toward Archie and Wolfe. Of Archie Cramer says he would like to have Darwin's opinion on him--"where were you while evolution was going on?" And he is just as abusive towards Wolfe, calling him a "fat bloated lousy liar." His carelessness with his cigars, which I should have mentioned earlier, is remarked upon--"He hurled his unlit cigar at my wastebasket, missed by a yard, and hit me on the ankle." But he still is willing to drink at the brownstone, having a bourbon and water on one occasion, and on another accepting Wolfe's "invitation to help with the beer, which he rarely did." Another cop we learn more about is Purley Stebbins: "He's not dumb by any means, and he has never forgotten the prize boner that Wolfe bluffed him into on the Longren case." [The Longren case, incidentally, is not in the canon.] Archie offers an explanation of Purley's ambivalent attitude towards him: "I am one of the few people Purley knows that he has not completely made up his mind about. Since I'm a private detective, the sooner I die, or at least get lost outside the city limits, the better-- of course that's basic, but he can't quite get rid of the suspicion that I might have made a good cop if I had been caught in time." And then there's Rowcliff: "If and when I am offered a choice of going to heaven or hell it will be simple; I'll merely ask, 'Where's Rowcliff?' We were fairly even--he set my teeth on edge about the same as I did his--until one day I got the notion of stuttering. When he gets worked up to a certain point he starts to stutter. My idea was to wait till he was about there and then stutter just once. It more than met expectations. It made him so mad he had to stutter, he couldn't help it, and then I complained that he was mimicking me. From that day on I have had the long end and he knows it."

Saul, Fred and Orrie all help out in this one; "Saul Panzer, small and wiry, in his old brown suit; Fred Durkin, with his round red face and spreading bald spot, in the red chair by right of seniority; and Orrie Cather, with his square jaw and crew cut, looking young enough to still be playing pro football." Saul, as always, rates a more detailed comment from Archie: "The only reason I wouldn't vote for Saul Panzer for President of the United States is that he would never dress the part. How he goes around New York, almost anywhere, in that faded brown cap and old brown suit, without attracting attention as not belonging, I will never understand. Wolfe has never given him an assignment that he didn't fill better than anyone else could except me, and my argument is why not elect him President, buy him a suit and hat, and see what happens?" Archie also says that "Saul can smell a liar through a concrete wall." Other regulars include Lon Cohen, who calls up to see if he can get any info on the case; Lily Rowan, who is merely mentioned as someone with whom Archie has "spent some pleasant hours"; Theodore and Marko, who are mentioned; and Fritz. Archie says that "Fritz is convinced that without him we would both starve to death in a week," and he reveals an unexpected side of his character when Archie has all those secretaries over for dinner: "There was a gleam in his eyes. 'If you need any help with all the ladies, Archie, for my age I am not to be ignored. A Swiss has a long usefulness.'" Why, Fritz, you old rogue!

PHYSICAL ASPECTS ::: A lot of familiar items at the brownstone are mentioned: the little table for check writing; the seven steps in the front stoop; the yellow chairs in the office; the big red leather chair, "off the end of Wolfe's desk, facing it"; the big globe "off in the corner"; and the couch, which Archie couldn't take in "from my chair at my desk . ... without swiveling or twisting my neck ninety degrees." The following gives us a pretty good rundown on the chair situation at the brownstone: "We needed seventeen chairs if they all came, and a phone call from Stebbins around four o'clock informed me that they would. With four from the front room, one from the hall, two from my room, and two from Fritz's room, Fritz and I got them collected and arranged in the office." That means there must be at least nine free chairs in the office. The warm room and the potting room are also mentioned. We are given a different phone number for the brownstone this time--PE3-1212. But the most notable new physical development is the pool table, which is mentioned for the first time in this episode: "The Sunday schedule at Wolfe's house was different since Marko Vukcic, his closest friend and the owner of Rusterman's Restaurant, had talked him into installing a pool table in the basement. It was now routine for Wolfe to spend Sunday morning in the kitchen with Fritz, preparing something special. At one-thirty Marko would arrive to help appreciate it, after which they would go to the basement for a five-hour session with the cues. I rarely took part, even when I was around, because it made Wolfe grumpy when I got lucky and piled up a big run."

ROUTINE AT THE BROWNSTONE ::: The immediately preceeding item should be considered a part of this section also. Wolfe's p.m. session in the plant rooms is mentioned. While we're in the plant rooms we should note a comment by Archie on the evening when the brownstone was invaded by a dozen secretaries, who naturally had to see all the orchids: "That was the first time in history that a bunch of outsiders had been let into the plant rooms with Wolfe not there. The awful responsibility damn near got Theodore down." Just a couple more items: Archie says "I usually answer [the phone], 'Nero Wolfe's office, Archie Goodwin speaking'"; and elsewhere he says "I wasn't supposed to leave a conference unless I had to."

ODDS AND ENDS ::: Only one item for this section this time around: "That January and the first half of February business was slow, except for the routine jobs, where all Wolfe and I had to do was supervise Saul Panzer and Fred Durkin and Orrie Cather, and for a little mix-up with a gang of fur hijackers during which Fred and I got shot at."

POCKET BOOKS CHECKLIST, 1-500
Compiled by Hal Knott and Marvin Lachman

1. James Hilton, LOST HORIZON
2. Dorothea Brande, WAKE UP AND LIFE
3. William Shakespeare, FIVE GREAT TRAGEDIES
4. Thorne Smith, TOPPER
5. Agatha Christie, THE MURDER OF ROGER ACKROYD
6. Dorothy Parker, ENOUGH ROPE
7. Emily Bronte, WUTHERING HEIGHTS
8. Samuel Butler, THE WAY OF ALL FLESH
9. Thorton Wilder, THE BRIDGE OF SAN LUIS REY
10. Felix Salten, BAMBI
11. Pearl Buck, THE GOOD EARTH
12. Guy de Maupassant, GREAT SHORT STORIES
13. Edna Ferber, SHOW BOAT
14. Charles Dickens, A TALE OF TWO CITIES
15. Hendrick Willem van Loon, THE STORY OF MANKIND
16. W. H. Hudson, GREEN MANSIONS
17. Ellery Queen, THE CHINESE ORANGE MYSTERY
18. C. Collodi, PINNOCHIO
19. Lord Charnwood, ABRAHAM LINCOLN
20. Thomas Hardy, THE RETURN OF THE NATIVE
21. Dorothy L. Sayers, MURDER MUST ADVERTISE
22. Johann Wyss, THE SWISS FAMILY ROBINSON
23. THE AUTOBIOGRAPHY OF BENJAMIN FRANKLIN
24. R. A. J. Walling, THE CORPSE WITH THE FLOATING FOOT
25. Robert Louis Stevenson, TREASURE ISLAND
26. Lytton Strachey, ELIZABETH AND ESSEX
27. John O'Hara, APPOINTMENT IN SAMARRA
28. P. G. Wodehouse, JEEVES
29. Charles Dickens, A CHRISTMAS CAROL
30. Anne Douglas Sedgwick, THE LITTLE FRENCH GIRL
31. Victor Hugo, THE HUNCHBACK OF NOTRE DAME (1)
32. Victor Hugo, THE HUNCHBACK OF NOTRE DAME (2)
33. Leslie Ford, BY THE WATCHMAN'S CLOCK
34. Jonathan Swift, GULLIVER'S TRAVELS
35. Percival C. Wren, BEAU GESTE
36. Alexandre Dumas, THE THREE MUSKETEERS (1)
37. Alexandre Dumas, THE THREE MUSKETEERS (2)
38. Agatha Christie, THE MYSTERY OF THE BLUE TRAIN
39. Edgar Allan Poe, GREAT TALES AND POEMS
40. Bruce Barton, THE MAN NOBODY KNOWS
41. Margaret Kennedy, THE CONSTANT NYMPH
42. THE AUTOBIOGRAPHY OF BENEVENITO CELLINI
43. Marie Belloc Lowndes, THE LODGER
44. Kathleen Norris, MOTHER
45. Rudyard Kipling, THE LIGHT THAT FAILED
46. Carter Dickson, THE BOWSTRING MURDERS
47. Frank Buck, BRING 'EM BACK ALIVE
48. Julia Peterkin, SCARLET SISTER MARY
49. Paul de Kruif, MICROBE HUNTERS
50. Earl Derr Biggers, THE HOUSE WITHOUT A KEY
51. Christopher Morley, THUNDER ON THE LEFT
52. Nathanael Hawthorne, THE HOUSE OF THE SEVEN GABLES
53. THE BEST OF DAMON RUNYON

54. E. Phillips Oppenheim, THE GREAT PRINCE SHAN
55. Thorton Wilder, OUR TOWN
56. Louis Bromfield, THE GREEN BAY TREE
57. Dorothy Parker, AFTER SUCH PLEASURES
58. Thomas Hughes, TOM BROWN'S SCHOOL DAYS
59. John P. Marquand, THINK FAST MR. MOTO
60. G. K. Chesterton, THE SCANDAL OF FATHER BROWN
61. Alfred Ollivant, BOB, SON OF BATTLE
62. THE POCKET BOOK OF VERSE
63. Jane Austen, PRIDE AND PREJUDICE
64. Mignon G. Eberhart, WHILE THE PATIENT SLEPT
65. O. Henry, THE FOUR MILLION
66. Enid Bagnold, NATIONAL VELVET
67. Johann Spyri, HEIDI
68. Dale Carnegie, HOW TO WIN FRIENDS AND INFLUENCE PEOPLE
69. John Buchan, THE THIRTY NINE STEPS
70. Philip MacDonald, THE MYSTERY OF THE DEAD POLICE
71. Ellery Queen, THE FRENCH POWDER MYSTERY
72. L. M. Montgomery, ANNE OF WINDY POPLARS
73. Erle Stanley Gardner, THE CASE OF THE VELVET CLAWS
74. Dorothy L. Sayers, UNPLEASANTNESS AT THE BELLONA CLUB
75. Lousia M. Alcott, LITTLE MEN
76. Dorothy Parker, SUNSET GUN
77. Ellery Queen, THE ROMAN HAT MYSTERY
78. William Macleod Raine, OH YOU TEX
79. Agatha Christie, MURDER IN THE CALAIS COACH
80. Booker T. Washington, UP FROM SLAVERY
81. A. A. Milne, THE RED HOUSE MYSTERY
82. Rafael Sabitini, CAPTAIN BLOOD
83. Patrick Quentin, A PUZZLE FOR FOOLS
84. Erskine Childers, THE RIDDLE OF THE SANDS
85. Dorothy L. Sayers, CLOUDS OF WITNESS
86. Carter Dickson, THE RED WIDOW MURDERS
87. Guy Gilpatric, MISTER CLENCANNON
88. Agatha Christie, THE A B C MURDERS
89. James Hilton, AND NOW GOODBYE
90. Erle Stanley Gardner, THE CASE OF THE SULKY GIRL
91. THE POCKET BOOK OF SHORT STORIES
92. THE POCKET BIBLE
93. James Hilton, GOODBYE MISTER CHIPS
94. John Buchan, GREENMANTLE
95. A. Conan Doyle, THE SHERLOCK HOLMES POCKET BOOK
96. Robert L. Ripley, BELIEVE IT OR NOT
97. Guy Endore, THE WEREWOLF OF PARIS
98. Mary Roberts Rinehart, THE CIRCULAR STAIRCASE
99. Ellery Queen, THE ADVENTURES OF ELLERY QUEEN
100. Charles G. Booth, THE GENERAL DIED AT DAWN
101. John Dickson Carr, IT WALKS BY NIGHT
102. Phillip Barry, THE PHILADELPHIA STORY
103. THE POCKET BOOK OF GREAT DETECTIVES
104. Emile Zola, NANA
105. Freeman Wills Crofts, SIR JOHN MAGILL'S LAST JOURNEY
106. Erle Stanley Gardner, THE CASE OF THE LUCKY LEGS
107. THE POCKET BOOK OF ETIQUETTE
108. THE POCKET READER
109. Ellery Queen, THE SIAMESE TWINS MYSTERY
110. THE POCKET BOOK OF BONERS
111. **David Frome, MR. PINKERTON FINDS A BODY**

112. Rex Stout, FER-DE-LANCE
113. Ngaio Marsh, ENTER A MURDERER
114. William Shakespeare, FIVE GREAT COMEDIES
115. Sinclair Lewis, DODSWORTH
116. Erle Stanley Gardner, THE CASE OF THE HOWLING DOG
117. THE POCKET BOOK OF MYSTERY STORIES
118. James Hilton, WE ARE NOT ALONE
119. H. G. Wells, THE POCKET HISTORY OF THE WORLD
120. Walter B. Pitkin, LIFE BEGINS AT FORTY
121. Mary Roberts Rinehart, THE ALBUM
122. Leslie Ford, THE SIMPLE WAY OF POISON
123. Robert Louis Stevenson, DR. JECKYLL AND MR. HYDE
124. David Frome, MR. PINKERTON GOES TO SCOTLAND YARD
125. Ellery Queen, THE TRAGEDY OF X
126. THE POCKET DICTIONARY
127. THE POCKET BOOK OF THE WAR
128. Omar Khayyam, THE RUBAIYAT
129. Van Wyck Mason, THE SINGAPORE EXILE MURDERS
130. Dorothy L. Sayers, STRONG POISON
131. Alexander Woolcott, WHILE ROME BURNS
132. THE POCKET QUIZ BOOK
133. Earl Derr Biggers, THE BLACK CAMEL
134. Ellery Queen, THE NEW ADVENTURES OF ELLERY QUEEN
135. Mackinlay Kantor, LONG REMEMBER
136. James Hilton, WITHOUT ARNOUR
137. Ngaio Marsh, DEATH IN A WHITE TIE
138. Erle Stanley Gardner, THE CASE OF THE CARETAKER'S CAT
139. Douglas Miller, YOU CAN'T DO BUSINESS WITH HITLER
140. Mary Roberts Rinehart, THE DOOR
141. Georges Simenon, THE SAINT FIACRE AFFAIR
142. THE POCKET COMPANION
143. Geo. Kaufman & Moss Hart, THE MAN WHO CAME TO DINNER
144. Max Brand, SINGING GUNS
145. THE POCKET BOOK OF MODERN AMERICAN PLAYS
146. Ellery Queen, THE SPANISH CAPE MYSTERY
147. Richard Halliburton, THE ROYAL ROAD TO ROMANCE
148. THE POCKET BOOK OF VEGETABLE GARDENING
149. Ethel Vance, ESCAPE
150. Faith Baldwin, THE OFFICE WIFE
151. Elliot Paul, HUGGER MUGGER IN THE LOUVRE
152. Dorothy Cameron Disney, THE BALCONY
153. David Frome, THE MAN FROM SCOTLAND YARD
154. Stephen Crane, THE RED BADGE OF COURAGE
155. Paul de Kruif, HUNGER FIGHTERS
156. Carter Dickson, THE WHITE PRIORY MURDERS
157. Erle Stanley Gardner, THE CASE OF THE COUNTERFEIT EYE
158. DAMON RUNYON FAVORITES
159. Jan Struther, MRS. MINIVER
160. Ernest Dimmet, THE ART OF THINKING
161. Zane Grey, THE SPIRIT OF THE BORDER
162. Sinclair Lewis, ARROWSMITH
163. Dorothy L. Sayers, HAVE HIS CARCASE
164. Patrick Quentin, A PUZZLE FOR PLAYERS
165. THE POCKET ENTERTAINER
166. Frances & Richard Lockridge, THE NORTHS MEET MURDER
167. Agatha Christie, PERIL AT END HOUSE
168. Earl Derr Biggers, THE CHINESE PARROT
169. Margery Sharp, THE NUTMEG TREE

170. William Kernan, DEFENSE WILL NOT WIN THE WAR
171. Phoebe Atwood Taylor, THE CAPE COD MYSTERY
172. THE POCKET MYSTERY READER
173. Edmund Taylor, THE STRATEGY OF TERROR
174. C. S. Forester, BEAT TO QUARTERS
175. Lloyd Douglas, GREEN LIGHT
176. THE POCKET BOOK OF QUOTATIONS
177. Erle Stanley Gardner, THE CASE OF THE CURIOUS BRIDE
178. I SAW IT HAPPEN
179. Ellery Queen, THE GREEK COFFIN MYSTERY
180. Carter Dickson, THE PEACOCK FEATHER MURDERS
181. THE POCKET COOK BOOK
182. THE POCKET BOOK OF AMERICA
183. Henry Lisk, THE RETURN TO RELIGION
184. R. Austin Freeman, THE SILENT WITNESS
185. Dorothy L. Sayers, THE NINE TAILORS
186. Helen MacInnes, ABOVE SUSPICION
187. THE POCKET BOOK OF DOG STORIES
188. Charles Nordhoff & James Norman Hall, THE HURRICANE
189. Ruth McKenney, MY SISTER EILEEN
190. H. C. Bailey, THE BEST OF MR. FORTUNE
191. Earl Derr Biggers, BEHIND THAT CURTAIN
192. James Reston, PRELUDE TO VICTORY
193. Eric Ambler, JOURNEY INTO FEAR
194. William Ziff, THE COMING BATTLE OF GERMANY
195. THE POCKET HISTORY OF THE UNITED STATES
196. Dashiell Hammett, THE THIN MAN
197. THE POCKET BOOK OF WAR HUMOR
198. Logan Glendinning, THE HUMAN BODY
199. Joseph Kesserling, ARSENIC AND OLD LACE
200. THE POCKET BOOK OF FLOWER GARDENING
201. Erle S. Gardner, THE CASE OF THE STUTTERING BISHOP
202. Ellery Queen, THE DUTCH SHOE MYSTERY
203. Joseph E. Davies, MISSION TO MOSCOW
204. Phoebe Atwood Taylor, DEATH LIGHTS A CANDLE
205. Daphne du Maurier, REBECCA
206. Marion Hargrove, SEE HERE PRIVATE HARGROVE
207. Earl Derr Biggers, CHARLIE CHAN CARRIES ON
208. Rex Stout, THE RUBBER BAND
209. Thorne Smith, TOPPER TAKES A TRIP
210. THE POCKET BOOK OF CROSSWORD PUZZLES
211. Dashiell Hammett, THE GLASS KEY
212. Raymond Chandler, FAREWELL MY LOVELY
213. THE POCKET BOOK OF TRUE CRIME STORIES
214. THE POCKET BOOK OF SCIENCE FICTION
215. Lloyd Douglas, MAGNIFICENT OBSESSION
216. Chas. Nordhoff & Js. Norman Hall, MUTINY ON THE BOUNTY
217. THE POCKET BOOK OF HOME CANNING
218. Rose Franken, CLAUDIA
219. Carter Dickson, THE PUNCH AND JUDY MURDERS
220. Donald Armstrong, WHAT TO DO TILL THE DOCTOR COMES
221. Ngaio Marsh, OVERTURE TO DEATH
222. Marco Page, FAST COMPANY
223. Erle Stanley Gardner, THE CASE OF THE LAME CANARY
224. E. Phillips Oppenheim, THE GREAT IMPERSONATION
225. John Hersey, INTO THE VALLEY
226. Nora Waln, HOUSE OF EXILE
227. Ellery Queen, THE EGYPTION CROSS MYSTERY

228. A. A. Fair, THE BIGGER THEY COME
229. Wendel Wilkie, ONE WORLD
230. THE POCKET AVIATION QUIZ BOOK
231. Carter Dickson, THE JUDAS WINDOW
232. Eric Ambler, A COFFIN FOR DIMITRIOS
233. THE POCKET BOOK OF CARTOONS
234. VOGUE'S POCKET BOOK OF HOME DRESSMAKING
235. Helen MacInnes, ASSIGNMENT IN BRITTANY
236. G. K. Chesterton, THE POCKET BOOK OF FATHER BROWN
237. Craig Rice, TRIAL BY FURY
238. THE POCKET BOOK OF MODERN AMERICAN SHORT STORIES
239. Mildred Hopper, HOW TO PLAY WINNING CHECKERS
240. Gustave Flaubert, MADAME BOVARY
241. Dashiell Hammett, RED HARVEST
242. Erle S. Gardner, THE CASE OF THE SUBSTITUTE FACE
243. John Steinbeck, THE STEINBECK POCKET BOOK
244. Walter Lippman, U.S. FOREIGN POLICY
245. Ellery Queen, THE FOUR OF HEARTS
246. Jonathan Latimer, THE LADY IN THE MORGUE
247. Martha Albrand, NO SURRENDER
248. S. S. Van Dine, THE CANARY MURDER CASE
249. Agatha Christie, THE PATRIOTIC MURDERS
250. Max Brand, DESTREY RIDES AGAIN
251. THE OGDEN NASH POCKET BOOK.
252. Erle S. Gardner, THE CASE OF THE DANGEROUS DOWAGER
253. William Irish, PHANTOM LADY
254. THE NEW TESTAMENT
255. THE NEW POCKET QUIZ BOOK
256. S. S. Van Dine, THE GREENE MURDER CASE
257. Leslie Charteris, ENTER THE SAINT
258. John P. Marquand, THE LATE GEORGE APLEY
259. Ellery Queen, HALFWAY HOUSE
260. THE POCKET BOOK OF GAMES
261. Agatha Christie, AND THEN THERE WERE NONE
262. THE SOMERSET MAUGHAM POCKET BOOK
263. Erle Stanley Gardner, THE D.A. CALLS IS MURDER
264. Frances Noyes Hart, THE BELLAMY TRIAL
265. A A F
266. Edward Stettinius, LEND LEASE WEAPON FOR VICTORY
267. Agnes Newton Keith, LAND BELOW THE WIND
268. Dashiell Hammett, THE MALTESE FALCON
269. E. C. Bentley, TRENT'S LAST CASE
270. Ellery Queen, THE DEVIL TO PAY
271. Cornell Woolrich, THE BRIDE WORE BLACK
272. Leslie Charteris, THE HAPPY HIGHWAYMAN
273. Robert Sherrod, TARAWA
274. Ernie Pyle, HERE IS YOUR WAR
275. James Hilton, RANDOM HARVEST
276. THE STORY POCKET BOOK
277. Erle S. Gardner, THE CASE OF THE SLEEPWALKER'S Neice
278. Margaret Carpenter, EXPERIMENT PERILOUS
279. John Hersey, A BELL FOR ADANO
280. Clarence Day, LIFE WITH FATHER
281. Neville Shute, PASTORAL
282. William Saroyan, THE HUMAN COMEDY
283. Ellery Queen, CALAMITY TOWN
284. THE POCKET BOOK OF ADVENTURE STORIES
285. Agatha Christie, EVIL UNDER THE SUN

286. Eric Ambler, BACKGROUND TO DANGER
287. Erle Stanley Gardner, THE D.A. HOLDS A CANDLE
288. David Lilienthal, T.V.A.
289. Craig Rice, HAVING WONDERFUL CRIME
290. Mazo de la Roche, JALNA
291.
292. Damon Runyon, TAKE IT EASY
293. THE POCKET BOOK OF WESTERN STORIES
294. THE POCKET BOOK OF JOKES
295. Dashiell Hammett, THE DAIN CURSE
296. Rose Franken, CLAUDIA AND DAVID
297. Ngaio Marsh, DEATH AT THE BAR
298. Jimmy Hatlo, THEY'LL DO IT EVERY TIME
299.
300. F.D.R.
301. Ernest Haycox, THE BORDER TRUMPET
302. Elizabeth Seifert, YOUNG DR. GALAHAD
303. Carter Dickson, THE READER IS WARNED
304. W. H. Upson, ALEXANDER BOTTS, EARTHWORM TRACTORS
305. S. S. Van Dine, THE BISHOP MURDER CASE
306. Ludwig Bemelmens, SMALL BEER
307. Anthony Berkeley, TRIAL ANE ERROR
308. THE POCKET BOOK OF POPULAR VERSE
309. Hans Zinnser, RATS, LICE AND HISTORY
310. B. M. Bower, THE WHOOP UP TRAIL
311. Faith Baldwin, WHITE COLLAR GIRL
312. Erle S. Gardner, THE CASE OF THE SHOPLIFTER'S SHOE
313. Ellery Queen, THE TRAGEDY OF Y
314. Thorne Smith, THE BISHOP'S JAEGERS
315. Mitchell Wilson, STALK THE HUNTER
316. Max Brand, FIGHTIN' FOOL
317. Lawrence Edward Watkin, ON BORROWED TIME
318. Paul Gallico, FAREWELL TO SPORT
319. Agatha Christie, EASY TO KILL
320. Raymond Chandler, THE HIGH WINDOW
321. Rosemary Taylor, CHICKEN EVERY SUNDAY
322.
323. Carl Crow, FOUR HUNDRED MILLION CUSTOMERS
324. Dorothy L. Sayers, BUSMAN'S HONEYMOON
325. Jack London, THE SEA WOLF
326. Ellery Queen, THERE WAS AN OLD WOMAN
327.
328. Philip MacDonald, WARRANT FOR X
329. Margery Allingham, THE FASHION IN SHROUDS
330.
331. Raymond Postgate, VERDICT OF TWELVE
332. Sally Benson, JUNIOR MISS
333. S. S. Van Dine, THE BENSON MURDER CASE
334. Erle Stanley Gardner, THE D.A. DRAWS A CIRCLE
335. Carter Dickson, NINE--AND DEATH MAKES TEN
336. Hilda Lawrence, BLOOD UPON THE SNOW
337. Clarence E. Mulford, HOPALONG CASSIDY RETURNS
338. THE SECOND WORLD WAR
339. Clarissa Cushman, YOUNG WIDOW
340. THE ATOMIC AGE OPENS
341. Agatha Christie, THE BODY IN THE LIBRARY
342. THE POCKET BOOK OF STORY POEMS
343. Roger Whitman, FIRST AID FOR THE AILING HOUSE

344. Irving Stone, LUST FOR LIFE
345. Eugene Cunningham, SPIDERWEB TRAIL
346. Frances and Richard Lockridge, A PINCH OF POISON
347. George Agnew Chamberlain, THE PHANTOM FILLY
348. Peter Field, GRINGO GUNS
349. Frances Parkinson Keyes, FIELDING'S FOLLY
350. John Dickson Carr, DEATH TURNS THE TABLES.
351. Ngaio Marsh, COLOUR SCHEME
352. Lloyd Douglas, DISPUTED PASSAGE
353. Arthur Henry Gooden, THE VALLEY OF DRY BONES
354. Mary Johnston, TO HAVE AND TO HOLD
355. Ellery Queen, THE TRAGEDY OF Z
356. Arthur Hertzler, HORSE AND BUGGY DOCTOR
357. Jesse Stuart, TAPS FOR PRIVATE TUSSIE
358. Chas. Nordhoff & Js. N. Hall, MEN AGAINST THE SEA
359. Pearl Buck, DRAGON SEED
360. THE STEPHEN VINCENT BENET POCKET BOOK
361. Craig Rice, HOME SWEET HOMICIDE
362. James Cliber Curwood, STEELE OF THE ROYAL MOUNTED
363.
364. Zelda Popkin, THE JOURNEY HOME
365. Anya Seton, DRAGONWYCK
366.
367. FAVORITE POEMS OF JAMES WHITCOMB RILEY
368. Erle Stanley Gardner, MURDER UP MY SLEEVE
369. Max Brand, SILVERTIP
370. Hervey Allen, ACTION AT AQUILA
371. Zane Grey, THE LAST TRAIL
372. John Dickson Carr, THE EMPEROR'S SNUFF BOX
373. Albert Payson Terhune, LAD A DOG
374. THE POCKET BOOK OF ROBERT FROST'S POEMS
375. Mazo de la Roche, WHITEOAKS OF JALNA
376. Frances & Richard Lockridge, MURDER OUT OF TURN
377. THE POCKET BOOK OF BABY AND CHILD CARE
378. Erle S. Gardner, THE CASE OF THE PERJURED PARROT
379. Howard Haggard, DEVILS, DRUGS AND DOCTORS
380. Faith Baldwin, MEDICAL CENTER
381. Richard Hull, THE MURDER OF MY AUNT
382. Howard Fast, FREEDOM ROAD
383. ROGET'S POCKET THESAURUS
384. THE POCKET BOOK OF GHOST STORIES
385. Joel Townsley Rogers, THE RED RIGHT HAND
386. Carter Dickson, SEEING IS BELIEVING
387. Lloyd Douglas, WHITE BANNERS
388. THE POCKET BOOK OF HUMOROUS VERSE
389. Raymond Chandler, THE LADY IN THE LAKE
390. Max Brand, SOUTH OF THE RIO GRANDE
391. Max Brand, THE LUCKY STIFF
392. THE POCKET BOOK OF ERSKINE CALDWELL
393. Elizabeth Janeway, THE WALSH GIRLS
394. Dorothy B. Hughes, THE BAMBOO BLONDE
395. Margey Sharp, CLUNY BROWN
396. Stephen Leacock, LAUGH WITH LEACOCK
397. THE POCKET ATLANTIC
398. Agatha Christie, TOWARDS ZERO
399. Darwin Teilhet, THE FEAR MAKERS
400. Eve Curie, MADAME CURIE
401. Thorne Smith, THE PASSIONATE WITCH

402. Rosemary Kutak, DARKNESS OF SLUMBER
403. Daphne du Maurier, JAMAICA INN
404. Ilka Chase, PAST IMPERFECT
405. Lloyd Douglas, FORGIVE US OUR TRESPASSES
406. Damon Runyon, RUNYON A LA CARTE
407. Erle Stanley Gardner, THE D.A. GOES TO TRIAL
408. John Russell, THE LOST GOD
409. Thorne Smith, THE GLORIOUS POOL
410. Emerson Hough, THE COVERED WAGON
411. Frances & Richard Lockridge, DEATH ON THE AISLE
412. William Wister Haines, SLIM
413. Conrad Richter, THE SEA OF GRASS
414. Erle Stanley Gardner, THE CASE OF THE BAITED HOOK
415. Daphne du Maurier, FRENCHMAN'S CREEK
416.
417. THE PETER ARNO POCKET BOOK
418. Somerset Maugham, THE RAZOR'S EDGE
419. Francis Iles, BEFORE THE FACT
420. Patrick Quentin, A PUZZLE FOR PUPPETS
421. THE MERRIAM WEBSTER POCKET DICTIONARY
422. Dorothy B. Hughes, THE DELICATE APE
423. Max Brand, THE FIGHTING FOUR
424. THE POCKET TREASURY
425. Gypsy Rose Lee, THE `G STRING MURDERS
426. Robert L. Ripley, THE SECOND BELIEVE IT OR NOT
427. Charlotte Armstrong, THE INNOCENT FLOWER
428. Thorne Smith, THE NIGHT LIFE OF THE GODS
429. Emerson Hough, NORTH OF 36
430. Gene Fowler, GOOD NIGHT SWEET PRINCE
431. THE POCKET BOOK OF FAMOUS FRENCH STORIES
432. Francis Iles, MALACE AFORETHOUGHT
433. Franz Werfel, THE SONG OF BERNADETTE
434. Craig Rice, THE SUNDAY PIGEON MURDERS
435. Bruce Marshall, FATHER MALACHY'S MIRACLE
436. John Dickson Carr, THE LOST GALLOWS
437. Ngaio Marsh, DEATH AND THE DANCING FOOTMAN
438. Erle S. Gardner, THE CLUE OF THE FORGOTTEN MURDER
439. Hilda Lawrence, A TIME TO DIE
440. Kathleen Norris, WIFE FOR SALE
441. Harold Bell Wright, THE SHEPHERD OF THE HILLS
442. Elizabeth Janeway, DAISY KENYON
443. James M. Cain, THE POSTMAN ALWAYS RINGS TWICE
444. Charlotte Armstrong, THE UNSUSPECTED
445. Faith Baldwin, PRIVATE DUTY
446. THE POCKET BOOK OF O. HENRY PRIZE STORIES
447. Thorne Smith, TURNABOUT
448. John Dickson Carr, CASTLE SKULL
449. Robert Benchley, MY TEN YEARS IN A QUANDRY
450. THE SECOND POCKET BOOK OF CROSSWORD PUZZLES
451. Agatha Christie, REMEMBERED DEATH
452. Bram Stoker, DRACULA
453. Kathleen Norris, MYSTERY HOUSE
454. Dorothy B. Hughes, DREAD JOURNEY
455. B. Traven, THE TREASURE OF THE SIERRA MADRE
456. Faith Baldwin, DISTRICT NURSE
457. Chas. Nordhoff & Js. N. Hall, PITCAIRN's ISLAND
458. Robert Dowst, WIN, PLACE AND SHOW
459. Ellery Queen, DRAGON'S TEETH

460. Patrick Quentin, A PUZZLE FOR WANTONS
461. Craig Rice, THE THURSDAY TURKEY MURDERS
462. Richard Llewellyn, HOW GREEN WAS MY VALLEY
463. Maysie Greig, DOCTOR'S WIFE
464. Erle Stanley Gardner, THE CASE OF THE ROLLING BONES
465. Agatha Christie, DEATH COMES AS THE END
466. Ernest Haycox, RIM OF THE DESERT
467. Brett Rider, CIRCLE C MOVES IN
468. Erle Stanley Gardner, THE CASE OF THE SILENT PARTNER
469. Rosamund Marshall, KITTY
470. Bess Streeter Aldrich, A LANTERN IN HER HAND
471. Ellery Queen, THE DOOR BETWEEN
472. F. L. Green, ODD MAN OUT
473. William Macleod Raine, UNDER NORTHERN STARS
474. Herbert Asbury, THE BARBARY COAST
475. Ngaio Marsh, DEATH OF A PEER
476. Craig Rice, THE CORPSE STEPS OUT
477. Giovanni Boccacio, TALES FROM THE DECAMERON
478. Carter Dickson, THE GILDED MAN
479. Thorne Smith, DID SHE FALL?
480. Kathleen Norris, PASSION FLOWER
481. J. R. Perkins, THE EMPEROR'S PHYSICIAN
482. Gwen Bristow, DEEP SUMMER
483. Daphne du Maurier, THE KING'S GENERAL
484. Henry Edward Helseth, THE CHAIR FOR MARTIN ROME
485. Agatha Christie, THE HOLLOW
486. A. S. M. Hutchinson, IF WINTER COMES
487. William Macleod Raine, THE YUKON TRAIL
488. Kathleen Norris, WALLS OF GOLD
489. Earl Wilson, I AM GAZING INTO MY EIGHTBALL
490. Thorne Smith, SKIN AND BONES
491. Max Brand, THE BORDER KID
492. Hilda Lawrence, THE DEADLY PAVILLION
493. Eric Knight, THE FLYING YORKSHIREMAN
494. Bill Stern, MY FAVORITE SPORTS STORIES
485. P. G. Wodehouse, CARRY ON JEEVES
496. John Gould, THE FARMER TAKES A WIFE
497. Mark Twain, A CONNECTICUTT YANKEE IN KING ARTHUR'S COURT
498. Pat Frank, MISTER ADAM
499. Rose Franken, ANOTHER CLAUDIA
500. M. J. Eher, THE SEXUAL SIDE OF MARRIAGE

MYSTERY*FILE

SHORT REVIEWS BY STEVE LEWIS

John Crowe, *When They Kill Your Wife* (Dodd, Mead; c. 1977; 217 pp.).

As all the inhabitants of California seem to, the residents of fictional Buena Costa county live in a world of intricately tangled relationships, the kind that too often result in murder. Even though they'd been separated for a year, when Paul Sobers' wife is killed, he's compelled to find out why, and a tightly closed corner of the world yields many secrets when the past has to be dug up.

This is an even more complex and tortuous tale than those that Ross Macdonald tells, and occasionally the going gets heavy. The ending is not fair to the reader, but while sometimes the finale to a detective story comes as a letdown, this one's better than any of the preceding parts, a triple-snapper! (B)

Michael Maguire, *Scratchproof* (St. Martin's; c. 1976, 1st U.S. publication 1977; 221 pp.).

In recent years Dick Francis has pretty well dominated the subgenre that combines mysteries with horse stories, but now here's Simon Drake, an investigator for British Turf Security, in the first of a new series.

It begins with Drake moonlighting as an advisor to a racing movie whose leading lady is being threatened, and of course there's plenty of shady racetrack shenanigans going on before it's over. Drake is crude but likable, and the mystery is agreeably complicated, but after the detection is over there are still forty pages of chase and rescue that seem to have come straight from a third-rate television extravaganza. (C)

John Buxton Hilton, *Gamekeeper's Gallows* (St. Martin's; c. 1976; first U.S. publication 1977; 192 pp.).

Few science fiction writers could create a culture more alien to us than that which existed in the rocky reaches of Derbyshire in the year 1875. Piper's Fold, a small lead-mining community reachable only on foot or by slow train, would naturally resent the intrusion of outside law in the form of Sergeant Brunt, whose unenviable task it was to find a missing girl.

The case itself should be an easy matter for most mystery readers, but they will be glad enough to be able to sit back in comfort while discovering the colorful sights, sounds and smells of what was, for all but the few, a rather mean and scabby existence. (B+)

Helen McCloy, *The Changeling Conspiracy* (Dodd, Mead; c. 1976; 182 pp.).

This unexciting rehash of the Patricia Hearst kidnapping might possibly have been redeemed by tighter plotting, but the adding to the cast of a newspaperman with a mysterious past, the CIA, and a renegade Mafioso does nothing more than cover over faulty logic and motivation.

Maybe the Hearst case could inspire an identical Connecticut version. Maybe the whole affair could be compressed into a week, including time for the victim to be brainwashed into joining her captors. The gaps produced by the murder of the kidnapped girl's father and the unexplained happenings in Chapter 5 are still left flapping in the wind. (D)

John Rossiter, *The Murder Makers* (Walker; c. 1970; first U.S. publication 1977; 184 pp.).

Retired Detective Inspector Roger Tallis, now independently wealthy, finds his craving to continue fighting crime satisfied by working for a secret agency of the British government and a man named Charlie. He's no angel, however, and there's not much other resemblance to that TV show you may be thinking of. When the hunt for an international drug sumggling gang takes him, the London sophisticate, to the frontier town of Shiloh City, Arizona, it becomes instead more reminiscent of wuite a different series, this time in reverse. But don't get the idea that Tallis is outclassed with a gun. There's enough sex and violence to please any television addict. No English tea shoppes here. (B-)

Ivor Drummond, *The Necklace of Skulls* (St. Martin's; c. 1977; first U.S. publication 1977; 185 pp.).

Even today India is large enough and mysterious enough to be the scene of a revived cult of religious fanatics called Thugs, whose sole mission on earth is to kill other men for their goddess Kali. The three intrepid adventures, Colly, Sandro and Jenny, stumble into the worst of it, and it takes many close calls before they escape, but not before a thousand Indians die, nearly unnoticed in an impoverished country strangled by overpopulation.

Although the last true pulp magazines expired twenty or so years ago, the kind of breathless romantic adventure fiction that monopolized their now discolored and musty pages can obviously still be found. Modernized, of course, and told by authors with more skill and more time for polishing their work, but it can always be recognized whenever a story is told for the pure fun of it. (C+)

Aaron Marc Stein, *Coffin Country* (Crime Club; 1976; 181pp).

I greatly admire Stein's free-flowing style. His mystery novels are always full of long descriptive passages that fill in the details of everyday events so well that you feel like a child seeing something for the first time. For example, while Matt Erridge's escape from being pushed into a tide-swollen gorge inside a smelly fish bag is not an everyday affair, even for him, it takes nine pages to tell about it. Want another? When the maid moves a button while Erridge is taking a shower, it takes him nearly three pages to locate it and to consider all the possibilities that its brief disappearance implies, and I found every word fascinating.

You probably know that Erridge is an engineer by profession, and for this particular adventure he's in Maine, up by the Canadian border, trying to determine if the famous Bay of Fundy tides could be harnessed for power without antagonizing any of the local conservationists. As it turns out, it was one of the latter who took an earlier, fatal plunge into Erridge's gorge, both facts naturally putting him under a great deal of suspicion, but with the friendly cooperation of a local Helen of Troy, his head somehow manages to survive all the beatings it takes--which should also tell you something about what kind of detective he is. (B)

Nancy Spain, *Death Goes On Skis* (Hutchinson/Crime Book Society; no date; 288 pp.).

It's Howard Waterhouse who's to blame for my reading this one, in a roundabout way. In one of his recent sales lists one of his offerings was a Nancy Spain book, not this one, with the somewhat diffident comment that it was "a bid different." Howard, that was as great an understatement that any book dealer ever made. . . . In trying to compare this one to anything similar, all I came up with to describe it was that it reads like a combination of P. G. Wodehouse and the original Nancy Drew, with a dash of Marx Brothers thrown in for good measure. It is, incidentally, dedicated to Hermione Gingold, whom I remember chiefly as one of Jack Paar's late night zanies, though maybe I'm confusing her in my mind with Dodie Goodman or Alexander King.

The central-European country that the Flaherte vacation entourage invades, complete with a company of friends and cousins, and a governess for a particularly nasty pair of children, is (would you believe) Schizo-Frenia, but there isn't a whole lot of skiing that goes on midst all the concomitant activities that perpetually surround a skiing lodge. There are two murders, however.

One difficulty from the trained mystery reader's point of view is that there is no detective worthy of the name for the investigation to focus upon. The local police are perfectly willing to hush everything up, although quite contrary to English custom the hotel does everything it can to publicize the unfortunate affair. Natasha, a Russian ex-ballerina who has appeared in earlier Spain novels, comes closest to being seriously interested in solving the killings, but alas she too falls into the spell that Barney Flaherte casts on all women in sight. The brilliant revue artist Miriam Birdseye is put forward by the dust jacket as the detective, but so far as I see all she does is loll comfortably about with Roger and Morris, her two gaily devoted male companions.

The author, and truth, have their way, however, almost as though an afterthought. As far as a recommendation is concerned, you'll have to give it a taste yourself, as I find affairs involving bitchy self-centered people wear awfully thin. What puzzles the most is how this mostly madcap business ultimately comes to have such a beautifully tragic finale. (C+)

Alex Saxon, *A Run in Diamonds* (Pocket 77657; c. 1973; PB edition, November 1973; 176 pp.).

In spite of my affection for Bill Pronzini's nameless
private detective, enhanced no end by his love affair with
Black Mask and the other detective pulps he collects, I do
find Carmody a much more original creation, seemingly more
free of the cliches of his particular sub-genre. Carmody
is a free-lance contact man, providing bodyguards, new
identities, black market commodities, what have you.
Since his divorce he has moved his theater of operations
from San Francisco to Europe and a villa in Majorca, which
is where this adventure begins.

    Stolen diamonds are involved, which should be obvious
from the front cover on. Somebody wants Carmody out of
the way for a while, and a wild goose chase takes him to
Amsterdam while dirty business is going on elsewhere. Carmody's business success relies greatly on his reputation,
and any embarrassment he receives he must take as a personal matter. And revenge he gets. A number of deaths
result, though not all at his hand. It's an earthy, violent tale, just complicated enough to keep you guessing,
and suspenseful enough to make one relish every minute of
successful retribution to the disrespectful enemy.

    Carmody has previously appeared in a number of shorter stories, in magazines like *Alfred Hitchcock's*, but as
far as I know this is his only novel. I sort of wonder if
Pronzini had put his own name on it whether this might not
have made more of an impression when it came out. Here's
the highest compliment I can give a book: this is the kind
of tale I would write if I could. (A)

VERDICTS
(More Reviews)

Emma Lathen, *By Hook or By Crook* (Pocket Books, 1977, $1.50).

The firm of Parajidans, Inc. is the largest Oriental rug business in the United States, founded and still managed by Paul Parajidan. Paul has four children, three of whom are adults, and who now own forty percent of the stock in the firm. These three are conspiring to take the company away from their father.

Paul's brother, who owned fifteen per cent of the stock, was killed in an accident, and left his share of stock in trust with the Sloan Guaranty and Trust for his sister Veron. Veron, having been in Russia for many years, had lost contact with the rest of the family, but has now returned to New York, where she is declared an impostor by Paul's daughter-in-law. Veron is poisoned, but the Sloan refuses to turn the stock over to the family until the question of imposture is settled. This brings the matter to the attention of John Putnam Thatcher, senior vice-president of the Sloan, who, as in other Lathan books, solves the mystery and identifies the murderer, but not before there is another poisoning.

The book is heavy reading in spots but on the whole it is a fine mystery. (Myrtis Broset)

Geoffrey I. Simmons, *The Z Papers* (Bantam, 1977, $1.95).

Secretary of Defense Kramer is attacked and wounded in Chicago while campaigning for the Vice Presidency. Kramer is rushed to the hospital where attending physicians decide he has been poisoned, but are unable to determine the kind of poison used.

The doctors later find a note, written on a laboratory report, declaring that Kramer has only 24 hours to live. As Kramer's condition deteriorates, other doctors and scientists are called in to try to find the cause of illness before the deadline set in the note.

Chicago police search desperately for the assailant, while Roger Thornton, TV reporter, chases down clues, with the help of his girlfriend, who witnessed the attack on Kramer. When another note is received, asking for the release of six men from prison, the search widens as police begin to investigate the background of the prisoners.

The medical details may be too technical for some readers, but the story, as a whole, is an absorbing one, as Kramer worsens by the hour and the doctors work to the point of exhaustion in an effort to save him, while the police try to track down the attacker, who is needed to name the antidote. (Myrtic Broset)

Georgette Heyer, *They Found Him Dead* (Bantam, 1977, 8th printing, $1.50).

A romantic suspense story.

When the firm of Kane and Mansell, in England, considers doing business with an Australian company, and

Silas Kane changes his mind about doing so, he is found dead at the bottom of a cliff. Silas's nephew Clement inherits his uncle's position in the firm, and when he too refuses to deal with the Australian company, he is found shot to death. James, the youngest Kane, and next to inherit, has two attempts made on his life.

A Scotland Yard detective is called in; he seeks for the murderer among Clement's wife's lover, the two business partners of the Kanes, James Kane himself and his stepfather.

James' fifteen-year-old stepbrother, his mother and stepfather add humor to the story, with the love interest being the companion to James' grandmother who falls in love with James.

The plot moves slowly but logically and is bound to hold the interest of all mystery fans. (Myrtis Broset)

Jackson Gillis, *The Killers of Starfish* (Lippincott, 1977).

A small-time ex-convict is shot as he leaves the ferry. In his pocket police find the name and phone number of Jonas Duncan, retired homicide detective. Jonas still has the same curiosity he possessed while on the Los Angeles police force and gets caught up in the investigation, though warned by police "to drop it--he is now retired."

The trail takes Jonas to the office of a real-estate promoter, a Skid Row bar, where he gets into a fight and feels sheer joy that he can still throw a punch, and finally to Starfish Island, where the killer finds another victim.

Starfish is occupied by Trevor Vance, and alcoholic and owner of the Island, Mrs. Vance, a chauffeur bodyguard and a housekeeper. Jonas is sure one of these people is the killer but the question is why. What did the ex-con know or see on the island that led to his death? Jonas has to fight his attraction to the lovely Mrs. Vance and not always having success.

The story has fast, constant action, with an unexpected twist at the end. (Myrtis Broset)

Robert Bloch, *The King of Terrors: Tales of Madness and Death* (The Mysterious Press, 1977, $10.00 [$20.00 signed], 202 pp.).

Here is the third book to be published by The Mysterious Press. This press, under the supervision of Otto Penzler, publishes first edition short-story collections by popular mystery authors. The first two volumes were a collection of Sherlock Holmes parodies by Peter Todd and a volume of Kek Huuygens stories by Robert Fish.

Robert Bloch is one of the few mystery authors ever to achieve equal renown in another genre. Bloch writes horror stories as well as mysteries; indeed, he was one of the original disciples of H. P. Lovecraft, and has the singular honor of being killed in a Lovecraft story. His first mystery, *The Scarf*, was published in 1947, his latest, *American Gothic*, appeared in 1974; there are about a dozen Bloch mystery novels, the most famous, of course, being *Psycho*. (There is also a "mainstream" novel, *The Star Stalker*, a novel about silent-movie days which is well worth reading if you can find it and ignore the misleading blurb.)

Although many stories from the mystery magazines have appeared in Bloch's sf and horror collections (*Cold Chills*, marketed as part of Doubleday's sf line, is half mysteries and half sf), this is the first Bloch collection to solely consist of mysteries to be published in sixteen years. The introduction is five pages of rambling commentary on psychotics, Bloch's mysteries, and changes in the mystery story over the years; then we have fourteen stories--twelve short stories and two novelets.

"Water's Edge" (*Mike Shayne's*, 9/56) is a tale of Rusty Connor, a bookie's helper, and the methods he uses to recover the proceeds of the bookie joint after the cops successfully raid it. For Connor only knows half the story of where the money is--and Helen Krauss, wife of a man killed in the raid, knows the other half--but she isn't what she seems to be.

"The Deadliest Art" (*Bestseller Mystery*, 11/58) tells how one-upmanship can lead to a deadly conclusion.

"Fat Chance" (*Keyhole Mystery*, 8/60) has thin John wanting to kill fat Mary--but his foolproof plan has a shocking way out.

"A Good Imagination" (*Suspect*, 1/56) is another method-for-murder story, as John Logan catches his wife having an affair with George Parker, and resolves to kill Parker. Parker is virile, but dumb, and thus very easy shooting--but Logan has a good imagination.

"A Home Away From Home" (*Alfred Hitchcock's*, 6/61) describes Natalie Rivers' return to England after many years in Australia, to an uncle she has never seen and a home that isn't quite a home.

"The Living Dead" (*Ellery Queen's*, 4/67) is a WWII story, as an actor pretends he is a vampire so as to provide sanctuary for the French Resistance--until the last act came.

"The Man Who Knew Women" (*The Saint*, 7/59) is the story of Luis Manuel, a.k.a. Lou Manning, a con man who marries old widows and then murders them for their money. Manning bilks Bessie Carmody out of $8,000, but his second attempt is both revenge and a commentary on the first. The story rolls along until the Final Shocking Twist Ending, which doesn't work; the rest of the story is good entertainment, though.

"Method for Murder" (*Fury*, 7/62) is a suspense story about a suspense-story writer, as the writer's psychopathic characters seemingly come alive to murder.

"The Real Bad Friend" (*Mike Shayne*, 2/57): George Pendleton leads a happy life as a vacuum-cleaner salesman--until his friend, Roderick, prompts him to murder his wife. Drive your wife insane, Roderick says, and use the insurance money to lead the beachcomber's life in the Caribbean. Thus Ella is faced with orders for strange produces arriving in strange quantities, rubber masks popping up in the window at odd hours.

"String of Pearls" (*The Saint*, 8/56): The string of pearls seemed so easy to steal--but one had to overcome the wiles of the East to get them.

"Under the Horns" (*Dark Mind, Dark Heart*, 1962): The worst story in the book, a dismal tale of death, sex, and revenge in and out of the bull rings of Spain.

"The Unpardonable Crime" (*Swank*, 11/61): The most dated story in the book, as Sherry, an actress, tries to restore her relations with producer ex-husband Roger in a small village in Mexico; "what she needed was a fix, but Sherry was through with Fixville."

"Untouchable" (*The Saint*, 3/62): Racist beefcake actor Race Harmon, filming on location in India, learns what happens if one breaks the local customs.

"Terror in the Night" (*Manhunt*, 2/56): Marjorie Kingston arrived on her neighbor's front steps, full of wild tales of bloodhounds, madness, and escape from the asylum --only the tales were true--weren't they?

As the reader can see from the summaries, these stories are tales of suspense, not of detection. Here are stories of psychotics and the asylum, told with a mordant humor: "'Don't you see?' she cried. 'It's the work of a madman. He belongs in the asylum!' 'My dear child . . . this *is* the asylum . . .'" This, then, is good-humored terror, the gentle "Boo!" instead of the abyss. It is as if the author wanted to scare the readers without offending their sensibilities, chill them without frightening them. Bloch's ability to fuse humor and horror is uncanny, but the two elements do not react well, and the reader should be prepared for a laugh instead of a shock. Bloch does, though, have a gift for characterization, and an admirable economy with words. His "twist" endings really do have twists to them, although one wishes that Bloch would restrain his tendency to end and title his stories with bad puns. The stories, then, are highly recommended, provided one accepts them for what they are and not for what they were meant to be.

The production of this book is quite high for an amateur press. The type is Baskerville, and easy to read; I could find no typographical errors in the book. The book is well-bound in sturdy black vinyl, and should last for many a year. Diane Cohen's cover is quite bad--pretentious and crudely drawn--but with the paucity of good mystery illustrators, it is as best as can be expected. A good, sturdy book, then, filled with fine fiction, and well worth your money. (A-) (Martin Morse Wooster)

Raymond Chandler, *Raymond Chandler Speaking*, edited by Dorothy Gardiner & Kathrine Sorley Walker (Houghton Mifflin, 1977, 271 pp.; originally published in 1962).

Houghton Mifflin has done well by republishing this fine book. Chandler wrote a lot of letters and the editors have taken many of them and divided them into sections: on the mystery novel, Hollywood, publishing, Philip Marlowe, etc. What Chandler has to say is often of great interest, as he was a fine writer. Also included are several articles including "Casual Notes on the Mystery Novel" (previously unpublished) and "Writers in Hollywood," plus an unpublished short story, "A Couple of Writers." The final section is the beginning of an unfinished novel, "The Poodle Springs Story", in which Marlowe is married.

Although this is better forgotten, the rest of the book is highly readable and extremely interesting. It's an absolute must for Chandler fans. (Jeff Meyerson)

Bill Pronzini, ed., *Midnight Specials: An Anthology for Train Buffs and Suspense Aficionados* (Bobbs-Merrill, 1977).

I was never a great train fan; maybe my indifference dates from my childhood when I almost electrocuted myself with an old Lionel set.

But I am hardly indifferent to good storytelling and this anthology has it. Best stories: Edward D. Hoch's "The Problem of the Locked Caboose," Cornell Woolrich's "The Phantom of the Subway," Ellery Queen's "Snowball in July," Robert Bloch's marvelous "That Hell-Bound Train," and a very fine original story, Barry N. Malzberg's "The Man Who Loved the Midnight Lady."

Pronzini is a perfect guide through these stories by providing clear, well-written introductions for each piece. In addition, Pronzini provides detailed bibliographies of more short stories, novels, and non-fiction.

This is a nifty collection you'll enjoy reading. (George Kelley)

David Axton, *Prison of Ice* (Lippincott, 1976).

Not long ago I criticized Dean R. Koontz's writing in these pages. *Prison of Ice*, written under the David Axton pseudonym, is another example of this fine writer's recent degeneration.

Let's tackle the plot first. The time is the near future when fresh water is an increasingly valuable commodity. One answer is to use the fresh water locked in the polar ice caps.

A scientific team is sent to test a method of creating huge icebergs that would float with the current until they drifted south where they could be towed to land. The method consists of using explosive charges to "break off" a chunk of the ice cap.

But, just as the team has set the charges, the ice cap is rocked by an earthquake (icequake?). And suddenly they, and the explosive charges, are part of a larger, floating iceberg. When the charges explode, they'll destroy the iceberg, sending the team into the icy waters. And, of course, there is an incredible storm going on so rescue is impossible. This would be enough plot for most writers, but not Koontz.

Let's talk about characters, because the subplots grow out of the interaction of the people. Koontz's first mistake is to throw too many characters at us too quickly: Koontz introduces us to *nine* major characters in 35 pages. That's simply overdoing it.

One of the characters is the son of an assassinated politician whose brother was assassinated as President. Sound familiar? The young man is writing for a magazine, as well as seeking adventure rather than the responsibility anyone with that famous name should bear. Well, during the bleakest moments, someone tries to kill the young man. Obviously, one of the members of the scientific team is a psychopath. But which one? The Nobel Prize winners,

the black, the anti-communist, etc.?
Deus ex machina comes in the form of a Russian submarine with a Captain brooding over the loss of his son to cancer. The whole Russian subplot is unconvincing.
So what we have is a book that has everything but the kitchen sink.
Parsimony in fiction, as well as science, is a good idea. *Prison of Ice* could have been a great book if Koontz had abandoned some of the subelements and concentrated on developing the characters, the setting, and thereby built the suspense that the book only promises, but never delivers. (George Kelley)

Patricia Moyes, *Black Widower* (Penguin, 1977, $1.95; first published in 1975).

I keep reading Patricia Moyes in hopes of getting hooked on her, but so far I have been quite unsuccessful. The last two of her novels I have tackled, *The Cocoanut Killings* and the present volume, have both been set, at least partly, in the Caribbean. It may be uncharitable, but the temptation is very great to suggest that Ms. Moyes depends upon the exotic locale to draw attention away from the insubstantiality of her recent novels.

Mavis Ironmonger, the white and beautiful but promiscuous and unruly wife of the black ambassador to Washington from the newly independent Caribbean island nation of Tampico, makes a spectacle of herself at a reception at the embassy and has to be hustled upstairs to her bedroom before she makes things even worse. When she is later discovered on her bead dead of a gunshot to the head it is only briefly thought to be suicide. As murder, however, it is decidedly embarrassing to Tampica, which is in the midsts of some delicate dealings with the U.S. about the future of an American naval base on the island and accordingly does not want to be in any way beholden to any manifestation of U.S. officialdom, not even the District of Columbia police. Since the murder took place in the Tampican embassy and thus on Tampican soil, the local police do not neet to be called in, but Tampica's own police force is so new and inexperienced as not to be quite up to handling the investigation alone. At length the Tampicans decide to ask for assistance from Scotland Yard, and Henry and Emmy Tibbets fly over from Washington for a look at things.

This has definite potential you might say, and you would be right. But Ms. Moyes just doesn't pull it off. The motive and means of the murder--and of a second murder as well--are ridiculous, the characters are almost uniformly unconvincting, and Tibbet's behavior is frequently incomprehensible. A very weak effort, altogether. (GMT)

Isaac Asimov, *Asimov's Mysteries* (Fawcett, nd; $1.50; first published in book form in 1968).

I am not one of that large crowd who enjoy disparaging the writings of Isaac Asimov. To my thinking Dr. Asimov's recent *Murder at the ABA* was one of the better mysteries of 1976, and his *Caves of Steel* and *The Naked Sun* are both outstanding mysteries as well as excellent science fiction.

The fourteen stories in *Asimov's Mysteries* are mostly science fiction mysteries. Some are not science fiction and some are not mysteries, but most belong to the hybrid school. The best of the collection involve that curious extraterrestrial scientist Dr. Wendell Urth, among which "The Singing Bell", "The Talking Stone" and "The Key" rank with the un-Urthly tale "I'm in Marsport without Hilda" as my favorites.

They are all light stuff, but what's wrong with that? (Guy M. Townsend)

Donald Hamilton, *The Terrorizers* (Fawcett, 1977, $1.75).

That I hold the Matt Helm series in very high regard is proven by the fact that I paid the full outrageous cover price in order to read this latest entry in the series without even a day's delay. I remember feeling outraged when paperbacks broke through the $1.00 barrier, and I am aghast at speed at which they have approached and are now breaking through the $2.00 mark. If this keeps up I may have to overcome my disliking for reading any books that I do not own and dust off the old library card.

Anyway.

Matt is back in Canada in this one, with a genuine case of amnesia which leaves him ignorant of his identity and with a bunch of baddies who think he's just faking it. But, though his memories are temporarily hiding out, his skills and capacities are still operational, and he manages quite handily to escape from the clutches of some wild-eyed revolutionaries who want to pick his brains. Later, after his memory returns, he is captured by them once again--just in time to foil their latest terrorist bombing scheme. Along the way Matt falls in love and plans to marry, but, as every reader of spy series immediately knows, Helm is not fated to enjoy marital bliss.

Though entertaining, *The Terrorizers* is not one of Hamilton's better efforts, in part, at least, because Matt just isn't pitted against worthy foes. A few SLA type punks with Syndicate connections just isn't the kind of competition faithful followers have come to expect Helm to deal with. Also lacking is the "if Helm fails the very peace of the world will be jeopardized" element which Hamilton frequently employs. Okay, so it's trite and corney, but it nevertheless adds some seasoning to the tales, and *The Terrorizers* could have used a pinch or two of spice.

The Matt Helm tales still constitute one of the best spy series running, but unless you are one of Hamilton's more rabid fans you might want to wait until you can pick this one up second hand. I wish I had. (Guy M. Townsend)

Peter Lovesey, *A Case of Spirits* Penguin, 1977, $1.95; first published in 1975).

Unquestionably, Peter Lovesey has the best historical detective series going in his Sergeant Cribb/Constable Thackeray tales. With remarkably few exceptions each entry is graced with wit and humor, fidelity to the late Victorian era in which they are all set, sound plotting, and fair play solutions to the crimes at hand.

A Case of Spirits is Lovesey at the top of his form. A risque painting is stolen from Dr. Probert's private gallery of nude works of art and the arrogant and offensive doctor calls upon his equally arrogant and offensive acquaintance, Detective Inspector Jowett of Scotland Yard, to get it back. Jowett, whose incompetence as a detective is matched only by his ego and his powers of self-delusion, turns the job over to Cribb and Thackeray, fully intending, as always, to take all the credit for himself when his subordinates have solved the problem.

In pursuing the stolen canvas Cribb and Thackeray are soon involved in the fashionable world of seances and spirit visitations, which enjoyed a considerable vogue at the time. They recover the missing canvas fairly early on, but they are then confronted with the more serious crime of murder--and murder in a most ingenious manner. But Cribb, as ever, proves himself more ingenious in solving the crime than the murderer was in committing it. Also as usual, Cribb takes pleasure in causing Thackeray as much discomfort as possible, whether by letting him sit out in the cold all night long on a stakeout when the suspect has been taken into custody by midnight, or by taking away the good constable's bag of hot chestnuts on the pretext that the person he has to follow will spot him because of their aroma. Thackeray's is a heavy load to bear.

But the reader's load is light and pleasant indeed, when it's a Lovesey mystery he holds in his hands, and *A Case of Spirits* is one of the best entries in this fine series. (Guy M. Townsend)

Erskine Childers, *The Riddle of the Sands*, with an introduction by Norman Donaldson (Dover, 1976, $3.50; first published in 1903).

One fall in the closing years of the 19th century, unpolished yatching enthusiast Arthur Davies is reluctantly joined by the sophisticated Carruthers for a boating vacation along Germany's North Sea coast. Actually, Davies thinks he is on to something which poses a threat to England's security, and he invites Carruthers, who is with the Foreign Office, more for his assistance in exposing the perfidious German scheme than for his companionship.

The Riddle of the Sands was Childers' only novel. Which is a shame, for he was a powerful story teller. Although the German plan which Davies and Carruthers uncover is quite difficult to take seriously and their amateur spying activities are almost embarrassingly simplistic, the novel is outstanding as a protypic spy novel. It is much better, in my opinion, than the later and much more highly acclaimed *Thirty-Nine Steps*, and its remarkably readable sailing sequences add immeasurably to its appeal. Indeed, the entire work is extremely well written and, except for an ending which limps rather badly, provides great reading pleasure even after three quarters of a century. That is high praise indeed, since most of the books written at that time are well-nigh unreadable today.

Norman Donaldson's introduction adds icing to the cake. He places the novel in its context, both historically and as a forerunner of the modern espionage novel, and

he provides a brief but feeling account of the interesting and tragic life of Erskine Childers.
 Our thanks are due to Dover for making this gem readily available. Of course, $3.50 is a bit steep .... (Guy M. Townsend)

Michael Delving [Jay Williams], *Smiling, the Boy Fell Dead* (Belmont, 1971 [1966]); *The Devil Finds Work* (Belmont, 1971 [1969]); *Die Like a Man* (Unibook, 1972 [1970]).
 The best part of these books are the titles.
 The three books feature Dave Cannon, a dealer in rare books, on his visits to England. Cannon tells a typical story from the "England-from-an-American-viewpoint."
 Unfortunately, the setting isn't well-presented enough to hold a reader's attention. The characters are dull. Cannon, of course, falls in love with a British girl and the romance is handled in a clumsy, heavy-handed manner. *Smiling, the Boy Fell Dead* lacks suspense; the identity of the murderer is obvious early in the book. All in all, a poor book.
 The Devil Finds Work gets worse. Cannon and his partner are back in England. They're offered a collection of rare books on the occult. The materials are owned by a man who claims to be a black magician. A servant of the magician is then found dead in a church, stabbed with a sword. Again, the identity of the killer is obvious. But the rest of the book is taken up with Cannon's partner's love affair. Yawn.
 The third book, *Die Like a Man*, is the best of the three. A strange man offers Cannon an ancient wooden cup he claims is the Holy Grail. Cannon reluctantly accepts it. The next day, the man is found dead, hanged and dressed in woman's clothing. Cannon tries to leave the Welsh town, but he is attacked and forced to remain in a hospital. Cannon manages to escape and this leads to the murder of a woman who attempts to help him.
 Again, the identity of the murderer is clear early in the book. The suspense, what little there is, comes from Cannon's attempt to escape; at times Cannon is completely overcome with paranoia, and with good reason.
 The Cannon series, with the flaws of poor characterization, transparent plotting, and clumsy style is to be avoided. *Die Like a Man* is listed on the TAD "Queen's Quorum Up-date." There must be some mistake. (George Kelley)

Max Collins, *Bait Money* (Curtis, 1973); *Blood Money* (Curtis, 1973); *The Broker* (Berkley, 1976); *The Broker's Wife* (Berkley, 1976); *The Dealer* (Berkley, 1976).
 I have a confession to make.
 Of all the varieties of crime and mystery fiction, I have an overwhelming weakness for the caper novel. I zealously guard my Richard Stark/Donald Westlake Parker series originals. I wait eagerly for the next shipment from England bringing me a dozen James Handley Chase novels unavailable in the U.S.
 So I began Max Collins' books hoping these caper novels would delight me the way the Chase and Stark/Westlake

books have.

I was disappointed.

Collins writes like Carter Brown, but without the humor. The pages turn quickly, but there is no substance. In fact, *Bait Money* is the only book of the five that is vaguely a caper novel.

Bait Money and *Blood Money* concern an aging professional thief named Frank Nolan. The idea is interesting; what would Parker, Stark's brilliant character, do at the age of 50?

But no, Collins doesn't explore this. He gets Nolan involved with the Mafia and in order to get off the hook, Nolan is ordered to pull a job within a month that will net him $100,000 so he can pay off the Mafia for killing one of its members twenty years ago. . . . Dumb, isn't it?

Well, Nolan goes to the Planner, a guy who sells plans of complete heists. Planner gets Noland to undertake a bank robbery with his nephew and his young friends. It gets worse.

In *Blood Money*, Nolan finds out that Planner is killed and his share of the loot from the bank job in *Bait Money* is gone. And he has to track down the murderer/thief. Compare this to Stark/Westlake's incredible *Sour Lemon Score*. Collins is in the bush leagues.

The trilogy, *The Broker, The Broker's Wife*, and *The Dealer*, concern a professional hit man named Quarry. No capers here either.

Quarry couldn't kill a fly in the real world. But Quarry acts like a character out of Marvel Comics, running around and killing people effortlessly. After killing his boss in *The Broker*, Quarry decides to go into a different sort of business in *The Broker's Wife* and *The Dealer*; he will protect the victim from the assassin. When Quarry finds out a hit is coming down, he goes to the mark and offers to keep him/her alive. Awkward. And much more dangerous than simply being a hit man. Unconvincing.

The real world of the hit man is presented in convincing fashion in *The Friends of Eddie Coyle, The Digger's Game*, and *Cogan's Trade*, all by George V. Higgins.

The Collins books are not in the same class as Stark/Westlake, Chase, or the early Earl Drake books, especially the underpraised *The Name of the Game is Death* (Fawcett, 1962) by Dan J. Marlowe. To be successful in writing caper or crime novels from the criminal's point of view, the writing must be powerful in creating a booding, paranoid atmosphere that pervades the amoral outlook of the characters. Collins doesn't come close to achieving this in his books, and they are much poorer for that reason. (George Kelley)

Richard Stark, *The Sour Lemon Score* (Fawcett, 1969, 160pp).

Nothing goes right in this entry in the Parker series. George Uhl, one of three other men in a robbery with Parker, shoots the other two and escapes with the money. Of course his mistake was not shooting Parker first, as he escapes and sets out to track Uhl down. He must turn detective, going to various people who knew Uhl and who may know where he is hiding. One of these, Matt Rosenstein, has Parker drugged and sets out after the money himself. Parker is cold and efficient as he moves from New York to D.C. to Philadelphia for the final, ironic conclusion. This is different from the usual Parker entry, as the robbery occupies only a few pages, but it's another fine entry in an excellent series. (Jeff Meyerson)

W. J. Burley, *Three-Toed Pussy* (Arrow, 1973 [1968], 187pp).
    Three-Toed Pussy was Burley's second book, and the first to feature his main series character, Superintendent Charles Wycliffe. Wycliffe here investigates the murder of Pussy Welles, a beautiful and intelligent, but somehow twisted, woman. She had most of the men in her small Cornish village in her power, either as lover or blackmail victim or both. She is found with one stocking torn off to reveal her deformed foot with its two missing toes. Disfigurement plays an important role in the story, two of the suspects being hunchbacked writer John Dampier and pub owner Mike Young whose face was badly scarred in a car accident. Wycliffe tries to soak up the local scene and its undercurrents, relying on Inspector Darley for the more routine tasks and clue-gathering. The village and characters are done well, and Wycliffe is an interesting character himself in his quiet way. Well worth reading. (Jeff Meyerson)

Richard Sapir & Warren Murphy, *Mafia Fix* (Pinnacle, 1972, 184 pp., Destroyer #4).
    This is the weakest of the Destroyer books I've read. There are too many killings and not enough humor. Remo Williams must find and destroy a huge 50 ton shipment of 98% pure heroin in Hudson, New Jersey. On the way to this goal he dispatches a large number of the local mafia in grisly ways. There is a little fun with Chiun and his soap operas, but it can't redeem the book. Not recommended. (Jeff Meyerson)

Aaron Marc Stein, *Days of Misfortune* (Doubleday, 1949, 190 pp.).
    Aaron Marc Stein's 1949 *Days of Misfortune* really wears pretty well. Set in Merida in northern Yucatan shortly after World War II, the story centers around the adventures of Tim Mulligan and Elsie Mae Hunt, American archeologists, during the *Kazil kin*, the Days of Misfortune. The *Kazil kin* are "extra" days, assigned to no month in the ancient Mayan calendar and are regarded by the local people with a good deal of dread; trouble comes during the Days of Misfortune.
    Trouble does come this time, bringing with it a series of murders whose victims are all tourists and/or intruders into the gentle, theft-free, spanking-clean life of the community. Because the chief suspect--Pablo, their pilot--is the close friend and associate of the scholars, the two undertake to solve the mystery. Of course, they succeed. Their efforts take them all over the area, and we become familiar with the town, the plumbing, the countryside, and some of the ancient wonders, as well as with

a charming array of inhabitants. Well, most of them are charming; the local people are. The Americans tend not to be.

For one thing, the American visitors we meet are not in touch with the local culture, and that fact symbolizes their aggression and lends tension to the book. It comes as a surprise to one visitor that there are still Mayans living in the area, "I thought they were all dead long ago." I suspect that this piece of information will come as a surprise to many readers also--it did to me--and it's one of the charms of the book. Stein packs fascinating details about both the ancient and the modern local culture into this short novel, and they lend a good bit of interest and excitement. In this way, the story falls into the category of mystery/detective fiction in which local color is used to bolster the story. It works here.

Another frequent device, the exploration of some kind of interesting profession for the central character could work here, but doesn't quite. Tim and Elsie Mae are labeled archeologists but they don't particularly *feel* to the reader as if they had special skills, perhaps because they're never seen at their work. Instead, they talk about their special knowledge, and we benefit from it, but if feels like a professional overlay rather than the real thing. Their archeology is only skin deep.

This small flaw is a part of a larger one, which is characterization. For the fan who demands careful, fascinating, multi-dimensional characterization, the book will be a shade disappointing. And that's too bad . . . the potential is terrific. Elsie Mae is, for instance, an independent and very capable woman and her professional reputation, we are told, is excellent. Tim, too, is well known, able and dynamic. The problem is that we *are* told; we don't feel it through detail and action. Also, it should be noted that though Elsie Mae is represented as self-reliant and forceful, it's Tim who gives orders and is the main sleuth here. Since we are given to understand that they have an easy, equable, equal working relationship normally, this factor seems a bit out of keeping.

The other flaw is the Catch-22 of the genre. Twice, we are set up for extensive explanations; both are conversations which spin out just a shade too long. The first occurs during one of Elsie Mae's few independent actions; the second, of course, is the final unraveling. In this case, Tim explains his reasoning while everyone, reunited lovers, police, friends, and killer stand about listening patiently. I've never been able to understand hou the killers could bear those scenes and just didn't make so much noise and confusion as to be led away. Being booked would be more interesting for them because they already *know* what happened. It's just the other characters and we readers (most of us) who need to be told.

Despite these factors, however, Aaron Marc Stein has done a nice job with *Days of Misfortune*, and it's good reading for the stationary traveler, the mystery/detection fan, or the Stein buff. (Jane S. Bakerman)

Octavus Roy Cohen, *The Corpse That Walked* (GM, 1951; Red Seal, 1957; expanded from the 1942 *Collier's* story, "Masquerade in Miami").

The creator of Florian Slappey and the neglected Jim Hanvey is unusual because he is one of the few authors whose early fiction efforts were published in the slick magazines such as the *Saturday Evening Post*, and several of whose last efforts, after a long literary career, were published as paperback originals.

The Corpse That Walked is better than the other two Cohen novels that I've read (*Love Has No Alibi* [1946] and *My Love Wears Black* [1948]), although both were published in hard cover by Macmillan.

Corpse starts with an intriguing situation when Alan Douglas, who is in urgent need of $20,000 to aid his fiancee's sorely troubled father, is approached by lawyer Wayne Hamilton with an offer he can't resist. He is to impersonate financier Lewis Hartley who is going to be busy with an undercover attempt to corner a newly discovered manganese deposit in South America.

Douglas has been selected for this impersonation because of his absolute honesty and integrity, and will be paid $100,000 for his work. However, there are two drawbacks: he'll have to undergo plastic surgery to change his face, and will have to leave his *fiancee* in New York while he lives another man's life in Miami for at least 3 months.

Douglas agrees to this proposition, but he doesn't know that there are a few extra hazards with which he'll have to contend. His employers seem to have somewhat lower ethical values than Douglas, and Hartley has a plan to avoid a forthcoming trial and jail sentence that involves an attempt to commit the perfect crime that will have Douglas on the receiving end.

Corpse is well-written, and contains a group of individual characters—some of whom are likable and attractive. Cohen tells his story in highly competent fashion, and propels it from start to finish without wasting any time or words on inessentials. He also avoids any excessive or arbitrary melodrama in his climax.

Corpse is not a major novel by any standard, but it is a solid, entertaining, and highly professional job of work. (Charles Shibuk)

Peter O'Donnell, *The Impossible Virgin* (Doubleday, 1971).

The fifth Modesty Blaise adventure pits Modesty, Willie, and the rest of the gang against criminal mastermind Brunel and his cohorts. Novikov, a photographic analyst for Soviet intelligence, discovers gold in an unexplored section of Rwanda. He defects, and is subsequently found, emaciated and tortured, by Modesty and Giles Pennyfeather, a doctor at a Tanzanian field station. On returning to England, they discover that Brunel has stolen papers that would seriously compromise British intelligence in the Far East if made public. Modesty and Willie Garvin must recover the papers and stop Brunel from getting the gold. It's a familiar story of vengeance and death, with the sentimentality of which we have grown so fond. Much the same as other Modesty Blaise novels, it's a good adventure, although routine. (B) (Martin Morse Wooster)

THE DOCUMENTS IN THE CASE
(LETTERS)

From David C. Ralph, 1420 Gay Lane, Lansing, MI 48912: Hate to start correspondence with a complaint, especially since *The Mystery Fancier* is off to a great start, again especially since I'm complaining about Steve Lewis, a great guy and a good critic. /// But, statements like "Unfortunately I find Maitland and his entourage of family and friends nearly insufferable bores . . ." are not good criticism. Good criticism (as distinguished from the personal invective kind of review so often found in the NY Times Book Review) either tries to resist personal bias or else confesses it and declines to evaluate the work in question. /// I know how hard it is to resist this kind of comment, and I also know that newspapers enjoy printing it and even demand it, but please, Steve, don't do it— especially not to my favorite characters! (personal bias admitted). /// PS. What is the "Crime Club"? I've hidden my ignorance too long. Is it a book club? If so, how do you join?
[*"Crime Club" is a special imprint used by Doubleday in this country and Collins in Great Britain for their line of mysteries. It really isn't a book club. "The Mystery League" (now defunct, I believe) was similar.*]

From Gerie Frazier, 7030 N. Bales #237, Gladstone, MO: Received *The MYSTERY FANcier* yesterday with great joy. Naturally I turned to your Nero Wolfe Saga first and enjoyed it very much. Library had a waiting list for Baring-Gould's *Nero Wolfe of Thirty-fifth Street*, but I finally got and read it. I thought it was good, although his theory of Wolfe's parentage and relationship to Archie was too far out for me. Also, his book covered only the stories through 1968 and I know of (and own) several written later than that. I really like your Saga the best--keep it coming please. /// Had to rest my middle-age vision, the smaller type calls for reading in short spurts, but I can handle that. I like the new format, the white paper IS best, and I'll go along with most anything that will help you to keep producing this high quality publication. /// After the Saga, I always read Mysteriously Speaking, then turn to the section of letters--you have a pretty good group out there! I was glad to learn from Dorothy Juri's letter and your comments about the two Nero Wolfe movies that were made. I had been born, but was not going to movies during the years mentioned, but Lionel Stander was around many years and I remember him well. He must have been quite young and was probably a very good choice for Archie. Wish someone could remember who played Wolfe --it tears me up trying to think of any actor in my lifetime that would fit the part. Hope they do make a TV series, if it is done properly we will be ardent fans. /// I have a thought about the proportion of men and women subscribers. I suspect that most women not working outside the home are addicted to the boob tube and don't read much of anything, hence are not fans of the mystery genre. Of the general population of female readers most are probably entranced with the Gothic Romances (yuck!), "intellectual" literature, the writings of the Women Libbers (P-U) and I hear a surprising number of gals are into porno--good grief!! What's more, I found your fanzine purely by accident in my search to buy Nero Wolfe books, so I still don't know how others know of the existence of fanzines. Most gals likely don't know that they exist. /// Regarding one letter suggesting that you omit your personal opinions from your Saga about Archie's racism and Wolfe's sexism, etc.--NUTS. I enjoy those comments, probably because I agree with most of them. It's darn near un-American *not* to form opinions and we are guaranteed the right to express them (suitably), so hang in there and do your own thing. Hope you do get the Saga whipped into book form, get it printed, and find it on the best seller list. /// Sure wish that I could help you out on cover art, but am devoid of talent in that line.

From Bob Briney, 4 Forest Avenue, Salem, MA 01970:
At times the cup overflows. A *Rap Sheet*, two *Nooks* and a *Fancier*, as well as the latest TAD, all in a single afternoon. To add to the fun, this was the afternoon that I picked up the latest *Rohmer Review* (#16) from the printer and had to start mailing out copies. The next *Review* comes back from the printer tomorrow, which is a signal that this letter has got to be written now. /// The use of white paper in TMF 1:5 is a definite improvement over the lavender-gray (oh, all right, lilac) of past issues. But, as you will have noticed, about a half inch at the right of each sheet refused to be fully inked.... Still, a definite step upward in legibility. /// All of the articles in 1:5 were much enjoyed, especially Jane Bakerman's interesting piece on P. D. James. The checklist of the Avon Classic Crime Collection is also welcome. I note two or three titles that I never saw on the newsstands when they first came out, and now must try to track down. (Incidentally, the question mark can be removed from the date on PN239.) /// I agree with Jeff Meyerson on the excellence of Gregory Mcdonald's two Fletch books. They were not, however, his "first two books". Mcdonald's first book was *Running Scared*, published in 1964 by Obolensky. It is still in print in hardcover from Astor-Honor, Inc., and in paperback from Avon (#31864, 1977, $1.50). It is a rather strange novel, but not a mystery in the usual sense of the term (whatever that is). /// Martin Morse Wooster's reaction to the third Mystery Library volume was, as usual, interesting. I avoided Rinehart's books for years, having heard everyone dismiss them with a "HIBK, feh!" Then I read her autobiography, *My Story*, and found it immensely enjoyable. This led me to sample her fiction (not just the mysteries), which I have found just as enjoyable, despite all the obvious faults. While it is nice to be labeled "admirable", Martin gives me too much credit for the appendix material in *The Circular Staircase*. All I did was suggest the set of extracts from *My Story* (only to find that Frederick Rinehart had had a similar

idea at almost the same time); I put this section together, and also sent in the list of film versions, cribbed from standard references. The rest of the appendix material was either commissioned or uncovered by David Hellyer, the editorial director of The Mystery Library, who should have the credit for the overall excellence of the assortment. Dr. Jan Cohn is on the faculty of Carnegie-Mellon University in Pittsburgh, and is writing a biography of Rhinehart. (In a non-mystery connection, she co-edited the "In Depth" section of the Winter 1976 *Journal of Popular Culture*.)

[*I hope that the inadequate inking on the right hand margin of these pages has been taken care of. It is one of my Gestetner 466's failings that it doesn't ink completely at the top of the stencil. Perhaps it could be fixed by a service call, but service calls are too bloody expensive. I have reduced the number of characters per line by 2 and have closed the pages in slightly; this should eliminate the problem. I hope.*]

From Jeff Meyerson, 50 1st Place, Brooklyn, NY 11231:
First of all let me say that I agree with you that there should be more letters in TMF. The letters section is almost always the first thing I read in the various mystery 'zines, for new information, questions and answers, people's opinions, etc. It's interesting to see what others are thinking and reading. I hope that Don Cole will follow through and update his High Adventure article; I for one would like to read it (having missed the original). On a question asked by Peter Pross, I don't think you can say that detective/mystery fans and collectors are synonymous, though many of us are both. I know many "fans" who love to read mysteries, some at an incredible pace, but don't collect at all. (They might buy books and then discard or sell them, borrow from friends, or use the library.) Many people do, of course, read and collect. I don't know of anyone who collects the books without reading them (though I sometimes feel that I will never catch up with new purchases), but I wouldn't be surprised to find that such a person exists. /// On the Pocket Books list, a list of PB 1-180 appears in the latest *Paperback Collector's Newsletter*. /// Mike Nevins is providing a very useful service with his ESG/Mason reviews. If he continues doing a few each issue we will shortly have a book by book rundown of the entire series. /// Since the Avon checklist appeared I've confirmed the date of *Death of a Doll* as November 1969. (Bob Briney also wrote to confirm the date.)
[*Alas, I've exhausted Mike's supply of Perry Mason reviews.*]

From Marv Lachman, 3410 B Paul Ave., Bronx, NY 10468:
I received TMF and went through it quickly, but enjoyably. Though it was a very rainy weekend in New York, it wasn't the rainy day to read Bakerman's article on P. D. James. I took your caveat and will hold off on the article till I have read James in her entirety; the one book I have read was quite good. What I did read was excellent; you are acquiring quite a stable of reviewers. /// Since several

of your letter writers were favorable to the idea of a list of the first 500 Pocket Book titles, I am enclosing a copy for your possible use. There are a few titles missing, but I suspect that these are titles which Pocket Books never issued--for some reason or other. If you publish the list, will you please give credit for it to Hal Knott as well as to me. I'm not sure if you know Hal who has occasionally written for TAD and the defunct TMRN. He originally provided the list for me to help me with my collection of old PBs. "Pocket" format of TMF is pretty good, and it is generally legible except at the end of some lines. Maybe I'm slow, but I don't get the front cover illustration. Is the continuing character (he doesn't look like a continuing character) about to be killed? [*Sure he's about to be killed. I think it's funny. What isn't funny is the fact that I'm having to re-cycle interior illustrations as covers. Are there no artists at all amongst us?*]

From Myrtis Broset, 204 S. Spalding St., Spring Valley, IL: Don't let Steve Lewis stop sending reviews. I am depending on him. This is the way I like reviews, short and to the point--I do not want to know the whole story. /// To answer Peter Pross: since Guy is publishing *The Mystery Fancier*, he should be able to tell you his basic purpose. I would imagine his intent is to share information, articles and reviews with his readers without going bankrupt himself. /// Yes there is a difference between a mystery fan and a mystery collector. A fan will buy books he thinks he might like, then toss it on a shelf until time for a yard sale, or will pass the book on to a relative or friend. Of course, the mystery fan could also be a she. /// Collectors come in two types. The first obtains books by their favorite authors. The second acquires any book that comes their way. These books are placed on shelves until there is no room left, then piled in boxes. Neither type will dispose of a book despite husbandly/wifely ire or warnings from a building inspector. Their only worry is which books to save in case of fire.

From Larry French, 14326 Milbriar Cr., Chesterfield, MO: Our "Pony Express" postal service has again accomplished the unusual in that I recieved my "preview" issue and Volumes 1-5 (sent via book rate mail) prior to receipt of your postcard (sent first class mail). Regardless, permit me to add my congratulations to the many others, in recognition of a monumental task *well done*, i.e. publication of TMF. If in any way yours truly can assist in eternalizing your efforts, please do advise. /// Although sufficient comment has heretofore been made as to the preview issue (a collector's item for sure) and volumes 1-4, I might, with your permission, add a few notations as to these issues, comment as to #5 and finally, pass on to you and TMF readers some activities in regard to John Dickson Carr, of whom I have read and studied for the past two decades and join with so many in being saddened by his death. (I have also enclosed an article on JDC for your consideration for publication in TMF.) /// First of all, I heartily approve of the new format (for convenience sake) and blatantly disapprove of complaints as to cost (thereby seconding the motion of John Ball in this regard). Your "Saga of Nero Wolfe" is excellent and closely correlates my efforts toward "The Grand Master of Mystery: John Dickson Carr", the same of which will be published and hopefully distributed later this year. /// Both Bob Briney and Mike Nevins (my fellow counselor and St. Louisian) adequately responded to your *Hag's Nook* (by JDC) inquiry relative to publication date, but I might add a few comments. *Nook* was Gideon Fell's first recorded case and as Anthony Boucher noted, Fell did seem a little muffled and not quite so ready to take center stage and dominate as he was to later (Dr. Fell, JDC"s most popular detective, although not necessarily that of JDC, appeared in twenty-three full-length cases, the last of which was *Dark of the Moon*, 1967). Boucher ranks *Hag's Nook* as one of Fell's best cases. /// In TMF 1/1, your review of Robert B. Parker's *God Save the Child* (his second "Spenser" mystery, published in 1974) is appreciated by another Parker/Spenser fan (this writer). I haven't seen his third book, *Mortal Stakes* (1975), reviewed by TMF, so will forward same at a later date. I have a review of *Promised Land* (his fourth, 1976, and winner of the "Edgar" for Best Novel of 1976) of which I am utilizing in a personal interview with Mr. Parker, currently underway. He was also featured in the "Chronicle" reprint, of which I thoroughly enjoyed reading. /// I, too, am looking forward to Marv Lachman's article concerning his theory that in virtually all of the Fell books by JDC there is one character who represents JDC. This leads to an interesting point that after the "Bencolin" books in which Jeff Marley was the continuing "Watson/narrator", JDC avoided such a continuing character although he would, from time to time, refer in a later book to characters in a previous book, i.e. Miles and Fay Seton of *He Who Whispers* (1946) being alluded to in *Panic in Box "C"* (1966). Rampole, himself, was present (briefly) in *Mad Hatter Mystery* (1933) for the express purpose of introducing a thereafter permanent "Fell" character, Inspector Hadley of the C.I.D. I had better add the fact that "Bencolin" enjoyed one final "curtain-call" in *Four False Weapons* in 1937. Thereafter, it was all Fell/Merrivale with Colonel March appearing in 1940 (*The Department of Queer Complaints*). (The question of whether Rossiter of *Poison in Jest* was intended to be considered a regular detective character is "answered" in my book on JDC.) /// In TMF 1/2, *Straight* by Steve Knichmeyer is reviewed by Jeff Meyerson and Steve Lewis and I herewith submit a "mini" review justified only by the fact that I would rate the book an average "C". The inaccuracy of Mr. Knickmeyer is proven by the passage on page 24, where "Straight" purchases a "whiskey sour" at Will Rogers International Airport in Oklahoma City. Such is impossible, in that "liquor-by-the-drink" is prohibited by law in Oklahoma and the particular cocktail longue referred to only serves beer (and 3.2 at that). The combination of detectives Cranmer and Maneri is remindful of Berkely Barnes and Larry Howe in Eugene Franklin's excellent detective series. Accordingly, the characters are appreciated, but the story-line quality hardly merits an "Edgar" nomination. /// In the same issue, Steve Lewis reviewed *Three Motives for Murder* (1976) by Roy Winsor. I had the pleasant occasion to interview Mr. Winsor (who is a former TV writer) this past summer at his home in Pelham Manor and I believe he is one of the finest modern-day writers in the Carrian tradition. His first Ira Cobb mystery, *Corpse That Walked* (1974), won an "Edgar" for Best Paperback Mystery of 1974. *Motives* was his second effort and *Always Look Your Bedroom Door* (1976) is his most recent on the popular bookshelves. I am looking forward to publication of his newest Cobb mystery, *A Sweet Way to Die*, in which a "Killer Bee" is the star of the show. /// Paul Shreffler, an English Professor at Merramec Junior College in St. Louis (and a fellow "Sherlockian") recently published an excellent interview with Isaac Asimov in regard to his *Black Widowers* in the St. Louis *Post-Dispatch*. He is also the author of a *H. P. Lovecraft Companion* (Greenwood Press, 1976). Phil presently serves as the Gasogene of "The Noble Bachelors of St. Louis", which features among its members Mike Murphy, noted authority on Vincent Starrett. /// As to TMF 1/3, I, of course, enjoyed the Nick Carr piece and the artwork of Fell (although Fell didn't have a goatee, walked with two canes as opposed to one and his hair was streaked with a white plume). I'll agree 100% with Steve Lewis in regard to his review of *Fletch* and Jeff Meyerson's review of *Three-Pipe Problem* (indeed, we Sherlockians love it). /// In TMF 1/4, again, the "Chronicle" reprint was excellent and it is noteworthy that the Mystery Library, an outstanding organization, has published a reprint of JDC's *Crooked Hinge* with a highly competent introduction by R. E. Briney. *Hinge*, of course, is a Haycraft "Cornerstone" and this exciting book about a "thumbograph" cites both E. A. Poe and Mr. Holmes as well as the great G. K. Chesterton (ironically, the three main influences on JDC's writings). /// In TMF 1/5, I (along with most Sherlockians) consider Hall's *Exit Sherlock Holmes* to be an excellent pastiche, considered in, of course, a light vein and thought-provoking to say the least. I reviewed it for BXM, but unfortunately, the review had previously been assigned. For E. A. Poe fans, read *The Poe Papers: A Tale of Passion* by N. L. Zaroulis (Putnams, 1977), which is an outstanding pastiche concerning certain previously unpublished manuscripts of Poe which are allegedly in the possession of a former love and anxiously sought out by a young Bostonian scholar. I appreciate the information provided by both Mike Nevins and Bob Briney in regard to the JDC "pulps". I continue to seek all that I can obtain in regard to JDC as he was indeed a most mysterious person himself. Accordingly, any reader of TMF having same, please submit. /// My pending JDC project is "The John Dickson Carr Memorial Journal" of which I "hope" to have ready for distribution by late fall. I further hope (depending upon response) to issue a similar "Journal" from time to time with valid assistance from Bob Briney, Mike Nevins and Jon Lellenberg. Any information, inquiry, etc. should be addressed to me at 14326 Milbriar Circle, Chesterfield, MO 63017.

www.ingramcontent.com/pod-product-compliance
Lightning Source LLC
Chambersburg PA
CBHW031428040426
42444CB00006B/732